# RUNNING WITH
# THE K

# RUNNING WITH THE KRAYS

## THE FINAL TRUTH ABOUT THE UNDERWORLD WE LIVED IN

## FREDDIE FOREMAN

### WITH FRANK AND NOELLE KURYLO
#### (AS TOLD TO PAUL WOODS)

JOHN BLAKE

Published by John Blake Publishing Ltd,
3 Bramber Court, 2 Bramber Road,
London W14 9PB, England

www.johnblakebooks.com

www.facebook.com/johnblakebooks 🔴
twitter.com/jblakebooks 🔵

First published in hardback in 2015 as *The Last Real Gangster*
This edition published in 2017

ISBN: 978 1 78606 280 2

British Library Cataloguing-in-Publication Data:

A catalogue record for this book is available from the British Library.

Design by www.envydesign.co.uk

Printed and bound in Great Britain by Clays Ltd, St Ives plc

3 5 7 9 10 8 6 4 2

Papers used by John Blake Publishing are natural, recyclable products made
from wood grown in sustainable forests. The manufacturing processes
conform to the environmental regulations of the country of origin.

Every attempt has been made to contact the relevant copyright-holders, but
some were unobtainable. We would be grateful if the appropriate people
could contact us.

John Blake Publishing is an imprint of Bonnier Publishing
www.bonnierpublishing.com

# CONTENTS

# GLOSSARY

At it – engaged in crime

Bird – prison time

Blag – con, cheat or rob

Coat off – deliver a humiliating rebuke

Dabs – fingerprints

Face – professional criminal

Fanny – sweet-talk or deceive

Firm – gang

Firm-handed – as part of, or accompanied by, your gang

Grass – police informer

Long firm – fraud wherein a former paying customer
disappears with a large order of goods

Moody – dubious, false

On top – apparent to the police

Plot up – arrive on the scene

Ready eye – robbery under police observation

Shillelagh – Irish ornamental club

SP – starting price, i.e. basic information

SP office – bookmaker's

Spieler / spiel – unlicensed gambling club

Tickle – proceeds from a robbery

Tom – cockney rhyming slang: tomfoolery = jewellery

Topped – killed

Verbal – uncorroborated written police statement

# FOREWORD BY TOM HARDY

So, you are asked to play not one but both of the Kray twins, among the most fearsome London underworld characters of the 1950s and 60s. Many people boasted that they knew the 'twins' but none of them had ever met them.

The sole surviving rival gang leader feared by the Krays is the notorious Freddie Foreman. Freddie was regarded as the boss of 'Indian country', meaning south of the river. The Krays would only venture across the bridge 'firm-handed' because of his fearsome reputation, but they had good reason to be respectful of Freddie and they built their empire upon many of the lessons he taught them.

So, how is it that this underworld enforcer has given so much of his time to coach me in the way the twins walked, talked, scratched their heads and even giggled? Well, Freddie was there and he fiercely believes that, if you're going to tell the story of gangland London, then you'd better tell it right. Because of his passion, I have had the honour and the pleasure of Freddie's company over the last few months to capture the essence of the twins, and, if I've managed to do so, it's because I have heard of their mannerisms, their characteristics, first-hand, straight up from a man who knew them before they both became killers.

Tom Hardy

# FOREWORD BY EDDIE AVOTH

Freddie Foreman is a gentleman and has always been a good and loyal friend. We have known each other for over fifty years and had some wonderful times together with our families – his children even call me Uncle Eddie

I first met Freddie in the 1960s at The National Sporting Club in London. He used to come see me box at different events over the years. I was the British and Commonwealth Light Heavyweight Champion with a record of 44 wins from 53 professional fights, 20 of those from knockouts.

I retired from boxing in 1972 and went to live in Puerto Banus, Marbella, where myself and a partner opened a high-class restaurant called Silks. Most of our clientele were celebrities and Freddie became a frequent visitor to my restaurant. A few years later, Freddie came to live there, where he became vice-president of the Marbella Boxing Club. He had a licence to put on boxing matches – 'Spain versus England' – he invited English boxing clubs such as Eltham South London Boxing Club to take part. I would often go to Freddie's Eagles Country Club, and sometimes we would go together with our families to Tony Dali's restaurant, or for a musical evening to Lloyds bar to hear one of the best voices in the business, Lloyd Hulme.

Freddie has been very generous in his support and help (both practical and financial) with my charities such as the Victoria Park Amateur Boxing Club, Ty Hafan and The George Thomas Hospice over the years.

# INTRODUCTION

Freddie Foreman has lived his life as an entrepreneur in the criminal underworld. His name has always commanded genuine respect (and sometimes fear) from those who operate outside the law, and even among those who uphold it. Freddie also acquired a fearsome reputation as a troubleshooter for many of the London 'firms' – most notably the Kray twins, who relied on him to clean up problems they created for themselves. Infamously, this led to a lengthy prison sentence as accessory after the fact to the murder of 'Jack the Hat' (Jack McVitie, 1932–67) – though 'Brown Bread Fred' continued to adhere to a strict code of loyalty that the Krays quite often flouted.

While known as the archetypal 'Godfather of Britain', Freddie has also spent time in the USA and seven years in Spain. It was from there that he was abducted by the Spanish police and brought back to the UK to stand trial in

April 1990 for participation in London's 1983 £6,000,000 Security Express robbery. Throughout his career, his criminal portfolio has also included major heists such as the bullion raid at Paul Street, Finsbury Square, in the 1960s, and allegations of gangland killings (which Freddie denies).

But, first and foremost, the career of Freddie Foreman represents the intersection of crime and legitimate business. He has owned or co-owned a chain of turf accountants, nightclubs, restaurants, pubs, gyms and residential properties. (At one stage, Freddie was even in partnership with the American Mafia to run gaming rooms in Atlantic City.) He has also lived as a man of principle, protective of his family and loyal to his friends.

We have known Freddie Foreman for many years now, having been instrumental in getting his 1997 autobiography, *Respect*, written and published.

'Freddie is a man on his own,' says Frank. 'There are two books about him on what he admits he's done, but you'd have to put ten books out on what he genuinely has done!

'He's an old man now, like I am, but when I stop down in London sometimes we go back to his flat for a drop of wine. That's when he tells you things: *Bloody hell, I didn't know he'd done that!* He'll shut up on you on one or two things he doesn't want you to know too, but he's a cracking storyteller, with lovely manners − if you didn't know him, you'd think he was a bank manager.'

Frank also operated in a similar respect with the late Ronnie and Reggie Kray, his recollections of whom are supplementary here to the unique Foreman anecdotes. This

Left-right: Noelle Kurylo, Freddie Foreman, actress Helen Keating and Frank Kurylo.

book follows the format of a photograph album; much of what you see here has never before been published. We hope the accompanying interview text will offer a further insight not only into the life of Brown Bread Fred, but also into the lives of his old associates, the Krays, whose legend stubbornly refuses to die.

Frank and Noelle Kurylo

# PART ONE

## BROWN BREAD FRED
## BY FREDDIE FOREMAN

I was born on 5 March 1932. This first picture was taken when I was two. I had rickets and they put me in the nursery to build up the strength in my legs. I was definitely undernourished because we were really poor, down in Sheepcote Lane, Battersea. Just the old gas mantles, no electricity, no real fire, only a stove to cook on, no heating. We'd got a radio with an accumulator, a battery filled with the acid you had to go out and buy. There was a toilet outside, naturally, and an old mangle for the washing – which I used to swing on with my mother. 'You're a strong little boy, Freddie!' she used to say, geeing me up.

We had a garden out the back. I was the youngest of five brothers – that's my brother Wally on his bike on the next page. We had a pigeon loft at the back and they used to go down to Battersea Bridge and nick the pigeons out of the bridge, which was a dangerous thing to do. My brothers Herbie and Wally used to go swimming down there, jumping in the Thames. Our father warned them not to do it, but as he came by there one day he recognised their shoes, so he nicked them and brought them home with him. Of course, they came home barefooted and got into trouble!

They were real hard times, real poverty. Then we got moved because just across the road was a railway with stables in front of it and the other end was a Gypsy camp with caravans. It was one of those areas with vendors coming down – you had the muffin man, salt sellers and knife sharpeners. Then there was Prince Monolulu: 'I've

got a horse!' The first black man we ever saw, he was an infamous tout. As kids we would follow him down the street; he'd have robes and a turban on. All the women used to run out and he'd give them a bit of paper with a bet on it. They all liked to gamble if they could afford sixpence, but he'd give the name of every horse in the race, so one of them would go, 'I've won, I've won!' One of the horses *had* to come in, that was his graft.

It was all tallymen then, having it on the never-never: sixpences and pennies to clothe the kids. In 1939 they moved us to Croxteth House on the Wandsworth Road. There was a row of houses and behind that was a big factory. We were the first people to move into this brand-new block of council flats at Union Road, Clapham, and we were delighted because we had an indoor toilet with an actual bathroom instead of the old tin bath that used to come out every Friday night – and I was the last one in, with all the scummy old water, being the youngest. But now we had a nice kitchen, electric plugs and a little fireplace. There were three bedrooms, too, whereas when we lived in Sheepcote there were four of us to the bed, top and bottom, and my eldest brother Herbie over in a little bed in the corner.

No sooner were we there than war was declared. The below picture was taken at the beginning of the Second World War. That's my father, Albert, and my mother, Louise, with me (centre) and my brother Bert (right) in Brighton.

My brothers had good jobs at the time, working in Whitehall Court as liftboys, wearing little uniforms. The

people who lived there would treat us to a hamper at Christmas, and to get a £5 note was amazing! We were just getting on our feet as the boys were bringing some money back into the home.

My father had been at the Somme. He served in the King's Royal Rifles during the First World War. A trainee blacksmith who was shoeing horses, he was conscripted at sixteen or seventeen. He got wounded in France: his arm was shattered and all the muscles were gone. As he wasn't strong enough to hold a horse and put a shoe on it, he lost his trade. He just walked around London, never had a bike, and learned 'the Knowledge'. So that's what he went into: the old taxi with the hooter on the side, in the open air, with a bit of tarpaulin in the back. That was a luxury, but the cab driver wasn't supposed to be comfortable! Out in all weathers, open to the elements. He used to bring the cab round to the flats and the kids loved the hooter. They would run and jump on the running board.

So, the Second World War started and then the air raids began. I remember the first air raid on Wandsworth Road – everyone was looking at the trails in the sky on a sunny Saturday afternoon. There was a dogfight going on up there, and it was quite an experience to see it. Then of course people realised what was going on: it had been a 'phoney war' as they later called it, up until the first raids came.

With my nearest brother, Bert (who was too young to be conscripted), I was evacuated to Woking. We were sitting in a hall; Bert was picked by a family and toddled off, and I was the last one left. I don't know what was wrong with me!

I finished up with a family, but it was dirty and rotten, and I had to sleep in a bed with other kids. The old man came in from the pub and never acknowledged any of the family, just went up to bed. One of the kids I slept with had TB – he used to cough up blood. It was horrible. I remember the woman standing me up in the sink to wash me, and I didn't like that. I was really unhappy there. After I'd had it good with my brothers all round me, Herbie, Wally and George had gone off to war. I was the youngest, and then there was Bert (above centre, on page 9 – after he'd joined the Navy), George (left), Wally (right) and Herbie (centre, bottom). Bert passed away during the interviews for this book, on 25 November 2014.

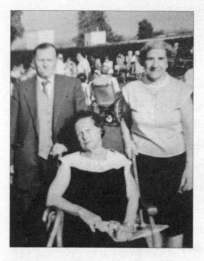

After that I was billeted to Brighton, with a nice, kind woman. That's my parents visiting Bert and me there, with my dad's sister, Auntie Emma (sitting), who'd lost a leg due to illness. I thought it was great in Brighton.

Then we went home and the Blitz really got started. All of a sudden I was in the thick of it. The factory on the other side of the road turned into a munitions manufacturer. We were sitting on a big target! They aimed for that every night – they hit it twice. Every street in the area was devastated. They used to train troops there because it was like a battlefield: all the conscripts with cap guns hanging on the end of their rifles, smoke bombs as hand grenades, even live ammunition. We were made to keep away, but we watched all the soldiers in the streets. It was like a game to us; it wasn't the real thing.

Across the road from us they put a barrage balloon and an ack-ack gun, and there were WAAFs (members of the Women's Auxiliary Air Force). You could sit at your window watching it, and on this one particular night my father said, 'I'm not going down that shelter.' They'd built one at the back of the house, you went down underground and there was an escape hatch at the end of it. You'd get

forty, fifty people down there in iron bunk beds. It was all right for kids to play and run around there, which I used to do, but as a family we wouldn't go down because there was just a corner with a bucket in it and a little sheet. It stank of carbolic.

All night long there were noises: couples making love and everything else. It was enlightening, I suppose; educational. But my old man wouldn't stand for it. We used to stay in the corner of the flat. In that one section my mother got all the pillows, covers and eiderdown, and put them all on top of us. That went on for ages.

But the Blitz got really heavy; it was coming down bangbang; they were trying to iron that factory out. We were in bed one night at the weekend and it'd just started. My brother Bert said, 'Come on, we'll have to get out.' I was still in bed, but all of a sudden there was an explosion! I was lifted out of bed and onto the floor. All the windows came in. Bert was saying, 'Come on, Fred, get your things on!' I was standing up on the bed and he was trying to dress me; I was only little. It was the first time we went down the shelter but we stayed from then on; it shook us up a lot. It went dark then. There was a pub across the road where my father used to play darts; he came home one night and it got a direct hit. They were all fucking killed, all of them local neighbours; he'd come home just in time.

I finished up being evacuated to Northampton, but Bert was old enough to join the Navy. Then there was a lull in the bombing and they thought, 'That's all right, he can come home now.' But there wasn't a family now: all the boys were in the forces; there was only my mother and father and me.

Bert was out in the Channel when they were attacking the torpedo boats that were sinking the Atlantic convoys; his ship got a torpedo in the bow. His captain said to batten down the hatches but there were still people down below. Dead ruthless, but they had to sacrifice them to save the ship. They got back to Portsmouth in reverse – they couldn't go forward with a hole in the bow.

Bert sailed around Australia and the Pacific. He saw a bit of action, though not as much as George, Herbie (whose wartime military record you can see to the right, which we're very proud of) and Wally. He was on the D-Day invasion, but George was on a ship sunk out in the Atlantic and the other two were in Paris. George's ship, the *Fitzroy*, went down in four minutes. We heard it broadcast on the radio

RS

**MINISTRY OF DEFENCE** CS(RM)2b

Bourne Avenue Hayes Middlesex UB3 1RF

Telephone 081-573 3831 ext

Mr A E FOREMAN
8A Alanas Avenue
Dundas 2117
New South Wales
Australia

Your reference

Our reference
92/52305/CS(RM)2b/10

Date
10   December 1992.

Dear Mr Foreman

In reply to your recent letter, our records show the following particulars of the
military service of 6847604 Private Alfred Edward FOREMAN - The Parachute Regiment

| | |
|---|---|
| Deemed to have been enlisted into the King's Royal Rifle Corps embodied Territorial Army and posted to Motor Depot | 15.11.39 |
| Posted to 1 MT Battalion | 12. 1.40 |
| Posted to 2 QVR Battalion | 29. 3.40 |
| Posted to 8th Battalion | 14. 3.41 |
| Transferred to Army Air Corps and posted to Depot *and School of airborne forces* | 22. 4.44 |
| Posted to 156 Parachute Battalion | 7. 8.44 |
| Posted to 1st Parachute Battalion | 10.12.44 |
| Posted to 12 Parachute Battalion | 7. 7.45 |
| Released to Army Reserve | 14. 5.46 |
| Discharged | 23.12.51 |

Cause of Discharge:  His services no longer required on proceeding overseas

Service with the Colours:  15.11.39 to 13. 5.46

| Overseas Service: | | |
|---|---|---|
| | North Africa | 18. 7.43 to 10.12.43 |
| | North West Europe | 14. 8.4  to  3.10.44 |
| | British Liberation Army | 8. 5.45 to 31. 5.45 |
| | India | 7. 8.45 to 28.10.45 |
| | South East Asia Command (Singapore) | 29.10.45 to 29.12.45 |
| | Batavia | 30.12.45 to  2. 3.46 |

Medals issued etc:    1939-45 Star, Italy Star, France & Germany Star,
War Medal 1939-45, Defence Medal,
General Service Medal with Clasp South East Asia

For details regarding replacement of medals you are advised to write to The Army
Medal Office, Worcester Road, Droitwich, Worcestershire WR9 8AU, advising them tha
your file is held in the EXE 49-51 collation, box 130.

OTHER MEDALS:   French Normandy          Yours sincerely
Dutch Queen Wilhelmina Cross
British Airborne Arnhem Medal

S C Mills

S C MILLS (Mrs)
for Departmental
Record Officer

by Lord Haw-Haw (the wartime traitor William Joyce): 'The German Imperial Navy today sank the minesweeper HMS *Fitzroy*. All hands were lost.' It was propaganda but there was an element of truth in some of it.

George was a stoker and he'd just come out of the stokehole in his boiler suit. He was making a cup of tea at the end of his watch. When the torpedo hit it capsized the ship. The ladder to the escape hatch was across the ceiling, so he had to clamber hand over fist to get out. 'Abandon ship! Abandon ship!' He didn't need telling twice, he just dived straight over the side. George was hanging on to a Carley float (a life raft supplied to warships) instead of a lifeboat. Another minesweeper picked them up, but he was out there in the Atlantic for quite a few hours. There were only a few survivors.

But we'd heard that all hands were lost, so we thought he was dead. I was looking over the balcony a few days later. My mother and father had shed plenty of tears, but all of a sudden someone walked over in a boiler suit, plimsolls and a raincoat. He waved his sailor's hat. I could hear my mother in the kitchen, washing the pots and pans.

'Muvver, quick, come out 'ere! It's our George!'

'George . . . *our George*?' She was drying her hands on her wraparound pinny as he came across the flats. We ran down the end of the balcony and there were tears. The old man went down the Portland Arms in the Wandsworth Road that night and they all had a piss-up. One minute we thought he was dead, the next he was alive. That's why I've always stayed close with George.

My brother Herbie was at Arnhem. That's him (second from right) at a memorial for the fallen in 1965. Ten thousand men went there; two thousand returned. Eight thousand were taken prisoner, wounded or killed. It was one of the biggest blunders of the war, Montgomery's idea – a bridge too far, as they called the film about it. They only landed with what they could carry – machine guns and light Sten guns – and a big battalion of Tiger tanks had moved in there. They had no chance.

It all went quiet for a period, so we stayed where we were right throughout the war, until the very end, when the V-1 flying bombs – the doodlebugs – started. Oh, fuck me, those were nasty! During the day they gave you a warning, you had to get to the shelters. On one particular day my father was on fire warden duty. You could always hear that drone, even if you were in the shelter, and then it'd stop.

*Oh, please, don't stop! Drop on some other poor bastard, not on us!*

Then it'd start up again and go a bit further.

*Oh, thank God for that!*

It was when it shut off that you were waiting for the bang, the explosion.

Down below, we felt the ground lift up. There was dust and all the lights went out. Everyone started crying and screaming. Some time went by and this one particular couple went up. They said our block of flats had been hit on the corner; our flat was right in the middle. My father came down, covered in brick dust, with congealed blood covering his forehead. My mother was all tearful.

'We lost everything, Lou,' he told her. 'It's all wiped out.'

All she had was this big old leather handbag full of her belongings.

Eventually we went up to look at the flat. Where we used to huddle together was just concrete. There were a few deaths – people who were in the building. We got sent to another address in Battersea.

I was evacuated again. My brother Herbie's girlfriend's parents had a shoe shop in Northampton; she had a nice old boy with a wooden leg that was just a piece of wood, not like what they've got today. Her mother used to say, 'Get that leg out the way!' and kick it when it stuck out – she wasn't very nice.

She got me working in there, cleaning the windows at the back of the house. I was looking over the back of the garden fence and I heard this woman telling her posh little boy he mustn't talk to me any more – 'You're speaking like he speaks!' – because I was a cockney boy. That was my friend gone.

Anyway, I was sitting on the windowsill; I rolled down the sunblind and fell into the main road! Right in front of a fucking bus! It stopped in front of me and I broke my arm. They put me in plaster and I remember how I liked being off school, getting a bit of sympathy and attention. I went to the cinema and the usherette said, 'What have you done to your arm, sonny?' I played on that, didn't I? The cinema was empty, it was freezing cold in the afternoon, but it was *Snow White and the Seven Dwarfs* and I really enjoyed watching that film.

I went back home and by then we were living down in Wickersley Road, off the Wandsworth Road. We had no furniture left because we'd lost everything, so they gave us this utility furniture made out of Lyon's tea chests.

My brothers were all overseas; they were in nine different campaigns from North Africa to Sicily and the European campaign, including D-Day. They all saw a lot of action and Herbie finished up in Japan at the end of the war, taking the colonial prisoners of war from the Japanese. So, even when the war was over in Germany, he was still out in the Pacific. They took a few of the fucking Japanese guards out when they saw what they'd done and the state of the prisoners. It wasn't properly disclosed but they saw the emaciation, and that they'd been chopping heads off with samurai swords. They found the store open and every parcel from the Red Cross was there; they hadn't given them to the prisoners at all. The prisoners were picking grains of rice out of the fucking dirt and the Japanese were giving it large in their smart uniforms! So, they chased them all round the camp and done 'em. But that story's not been told.

This was after the war, about 1948. I think there might be a drop of foreign blood in me. My mother was very dark, with long black hair, but my brother George is blond and blue-eyed so I don't know what my mother was up to, years ago! These two are young guys I used to knock around with (Billy Adams – left – and Joe Turner at the Roehampton open-air swimming pool); one of them is dead now and I don't know about the other one.

Recently, I went back to my roots at the Battersea Boxing Club, at the Latchmere pub, where I had quite a few amateur fights. We used to fight the Army, the Navy, the Police Force, Nine Elms baths and Tooting Bec baths – they used the baths as boxing arenas for the amateur shows. I belonged to Jack Solomon's Nursery. His gymnasium was above a snooker hall in Windmill Street, Soho; there was a salt-beef bar underneath it. My old man and my brothers used to come to watch me box. At Jack Solomon's on a Sunday morning you used to see all the top fighters coming over from America to fight Bruce Woodcock and Freddie Mills. We were really into all that. We'd listen to all the fights on the crystal set back in Sheepcote Lane, like when Tommy Farr fought Joe Louis – we thought he'd won it because it sounded like he had by the commentary, but he didn't get the decision. Boxing was the main sporting interest then rather than football, but Chelsea were just over the bridge and my brothers used to support them.

In those days, every Saturday night there would be a fight outside the pub; blood on the cobbles. They'd all form a circle, and my old man used to fight this guy called Johnny Whicker. He had loads of fights with him and it was, 'Who's going to fucking win this one?' It was a real rivalry between the two of them. Whicker was half-related to the family; he was someone's husband. But, even when we used to have a party at Sheepcote Lane, they'd be all round the piano, singing and drinking – then they'd be screaming and hollering. It'd be the old man and Johnny Whicker having a straightener outside the door. I can remember watching them roll around the ground, punching each other.

But boxing was just learning how to defend yourself and boxers were the heroes of the day. Herbie got involved in boxing and 'Boy' Bessell, an area champion, used to come from Bristol to visit us, so that was another incentive for teaching you how to shape up. Jack Sullivan was famous then, and he was the reason why I joined Battersea Boxing Club. When I went over to Solomon's gym with all the professionals, my father and his friends would come and sit on these trestles to watch them sparring, training and working out.

I used to go to Bud Flanagan's Crazy Gang Show at the Victoria Palace because he would sponsor the young boxers. Flanagan had a little place just round the corner and it was the first fucking time I'd been to a restaurant! He treated us all to a bowl of tomato soup, all the junior boys. The film actor Stewart Granger used to come up there as a sponsor – he bought me these shorts with the 'FF' on (see next page). I trained indoors; my brothers had weights lying around and I used them too.

I can remember fighting on the undercard at Manor Place Baths. I never had a dressing gown or anything like that. Henry Cooper, George Cooper, Dave Charnley, Charlie Tucker and Freddie Reardon were on the bill – all local fighters from south London. It was Henry Cooper's first pro fight. Tommy Davey was the manager and he'd overmatched me with Del Breen from Croydon because this guy had had twenty fucking fights and won the last four on knockout! It was my first pro fight, so Davey tried to talk me out of it. I said, 'I've told everyone I'm fighting now, I've gotta be on the bill!'

Because I had a lot of friends and supporters I used to have a lot of fights over the coffee stalls. I'd bring blokes over to have a row with me – up at the Elephant & Castle, Tooting, World's End, I used to go there just to have a fight.

'Who's the best fighter you've got round 'ere?'

I pushed up the front but I was fighting full-grown men, not teenagers. I was scaffolding, saddling roofs and I'd

worked in Smithfield meat market, carrying sides of beef about in cold stores, so I was a pretty strong kid. It was hard fucking graft – I did it just to earn a few quid extra.

But this night I was the first one on. I rushed there and got in the ring, just in my shorts and a towel. As the bell went I charged out to have a row, tripped over his foot and hit the ropes. I remember the crowd laughing. Though I didn't go down, it made me feel a bit silly, gave me the hump; I suppose it was a bit comical. But then I got serious. We had six rounds of three minutes, which was a lot for a first fight. But I had a right fucking war! In the third round, I came out with some really good shots and put him down. I thought, 'I've won this' but at the end of the round the fucking bell saved him – they had to pick him up and put him in his corner.

After the fight, the 'nobbings' started coming in the ring – half a crown, silver. I was paid twelve quid for the fight but got about twenty-odd quid nobbings. So did Del Breen, and that was money then. I got good write-ups in *The Ring* and *Boxing News*, and this was with top-rated fighters and future champions on the bill.

The guy in my corner later said, 'I could have made a champion out of Fred.' Henry Cooper's manager, Jim Wicks, declared, 'He'll never get an easy fight now, because he can't be matched with novices like himself.' I'd had twenty or thirty fights as an amateur, and I had a following of girls, all screaming their heads off. I liked the little bit of notoriety, of course, and it didn't stop me pulling a few girls, either – they were a perk of the job. But Wicks turned out to be right.

Then I got into thieving and that was easy money. Why get your brain scrambled for twelve or twenty quid when you can get a hundred quid out of thieving? I was nicking washing machines, spin dryers and Hoovers; when televisions started coming on the market, we were picking open the shops on half-day closing and going in there.

With the boxing I might have made it, I might not. You just don't know, do you?

The picture overleaf (left) is me with my old girlfriend, Patsy Keith. She was a bookmaker's daughter, a lovely girl. We had a little fling. Then I met my Maureen – that's her on the motorcycle, the woman I married, with our Gregory at a year old. She got pregnant, so it was a bit of a fucking shotgun wedding!

Milton Road was in Herne Hill – all the streets up there are named after the poets. We got a little ground-floor flat there. The girls in those days, they entrapped you, they set their sights on you: he's a little bit of a money-getter, he keeps coming up in taxis and picking me up . . . She was working in a factory, pressing women's clothes, so she stopped work from that day onwards! The next thing I know I'm getting married, we're getting the bottom drawer ready.

I was nineteen. Before that I'd already been in the nick: at sixteen I was nicked for affray after a gang fight – I was dragged into this retaliation by some kids who'd got beaten up. There was a boys' club over on the North Dulwich–Peckham border; it was a rough area. Two mates of mine who used to go to the dancehalls had been battered by a mob out of the club. We had a bit of a skirmish and, the next thing you know, I'm fucking nicked! Nobody got hurt really badly, it was just the fact that these kids from Clapham had come over and had a fight in the street. It finished up in the club itself. We had a sand-weighted sock as a cosh!

There were six of us from Clapham who ended up at the

Old Bailey. It was ridiculous, really; it went on for over a week. One of the prosecution would hold up this smelly old sock away from his nose and say, '. . . and one sand-weighted sock.' We used to have our heads down, but we'd repeat it, giggling every time he said it: '. . . and one sand-weighted sock!' We all got fined a fiver. Sir Gerald Dodson was the judge and he gave us a right lecture: 'When you walk out of here, look up at the sky. If you go on like this, you're going to wind up doing prison time.' As if we didn't know what a cell was: we'd been in the fucking Old Bailey cells for a week!

But I was sent to Stamford House, the remand centre at Shepherd's Bush. It was known throughout the criminal fraternity – for years to come all the London villains I met in prisons up and down the country started off in Stamford House. It was a breeding ground for crime, this gaff; it hardened you.

This is me with Tommy Wisbey (overleaf, top picture), later one of the Great Train Robbers, whom I've known since I was fifteen or sixteen, and a little team. The chauffeur/driver took us down to the hop country in Kent to have a drink and a night out. There's another picture of us below. Later on, I'd be godfather to his daughter, Marilyn. Tommy would lose his other daughter, Lorraine, while he was away: she was killed in a car crash. She was only sixteen.

I had Tommy on the firm with me when we'd go rob the shops in Clapham on closing day: Wednesday or Thursday afternoon, that's how it used to be in those days. 'The Bosh' was the guy who would make all the keys for you in

alphabetical order and you used to keep trying them out till one threw the lock over. They were usually double-throw locks. Then we could walk in, walk round, come back and lock it up, then go to the end of the street to see if it was belled to the nick. Because there weren't bells like there are today; people didn't think it was necessary. I'd say 90 per cent of them had no alarms.

We used to pull up in a van. I'd have a brown coat on and we would be 'the workers', carrying out the washing machines and radiograms over the pavement. We'd load up the van and we had them already sold. We'd fill out the orders: 'My daughter's getting married, can you get her a Hoover cleaner?' That was how we performed.

Tommy's still alive, though his wife, Rene, has just died. Rene was my Maureen's friend: 'I've found a nice fella for you!' Girls look after their mates, they plot and plan and scheme – and ensnare you. To not get married in the fifties when you got a girl pregnant, you were the dirtiest dog ever!

At this time I went and bought this big old car (below) at the sale. You can see the ladder on the roof rack. This guy on the right, a Paddy, was the labourer; the guy on the far left

was an electrician and a plumber, and my pal Horry Dance and myself were both thieves. We used to nick all the paint and all the materials, so we were alright for a bit of painting and decorating. We had a few contacts, and anything they wanted I'd go out and nick.

We ran the painting-and-decorating firm for a couple of years; this is outside the house in Elsynge Road that Horry bought (he finished up buying about three houses). He carried on but I left it and sold the motor to my brother-in-law.

The family had bucket-and-sponge days at all the racetracks and dog tracks. Maureen's uncle took bets under the name Jack Ray; he was the first one to have a telephone, which he'd work with his feet, and put up runners from other racetracks on the board. It was all bollocks, because he was making his own prices up. He was a shrewd bastard, Jack! But he got five years for assault and got the birch – so he was a face. Gordon Goody, Tommy Wisbey and Buster Edwards got it in Wormwood Scrubs too – they'd stand you up against a cross and bind the birch twigs up into a whip. Prisons were brutal at that time.

It had been a short period of trying to go straight but afterwards I took Tommy with me. Buster Edwards had just come out of the RAF and tried a window-cleaning business; that went pear-shaped, so he went to work for a florist called A.D. Warner in Lower Marsh, The Cut. He used to sell our goods for us to the stallholders. When he saw the sort of money we were making, he said, 'Can't I come to work for you?' So I turned him into a fucking criminal because he was previously a straight-goer.

Tommy Wisbey's father used to stand on the corner of Cooks Road, Kennington, taking illegal bets. The coppers would run him down the nick for street bookmaking. He'd have to produce bodies for them: pay people to get nicked at Lambeth Court. I even did it myself once: all you did was take a few slips in your pocket, the copper took you in the nick and charged you. That was the crooked little coup. They had their lookouts. They came round as milkmen and coalmen; it was a game to a lot of them. Tommy's old man had a bottle-washing yard and whoever was taking the bets used to go through the yard to escape.

So, Tommy, Buster and I were the main three during that period. We took a big van down to Southampton because we wanted to do this particular electrical supplier. We did it early morning so we could get back to London; we emptied the shop out – there was no one there – and put it all on the van. We loaded up and pulled off and then Tommy comes up the other side and tells us to pull over. We had a crooked Ford Zephyr to escort the van.

'What's the matter?'

We had a Decca radiogram that you screwed legs onto the bottom of; it was a great little seller. 'That Decca,' he said, 'I've fuckin' handled that!' He meant his dabs would be on it, because we couldn't walk across the pavement with gloves on. If two coppers walked by, chatting, I'd say, 'Don't worry, just keep normal.' But it meant your dabs were on the gear you'd nicked.

'I fuckin' left it inside the door. I forgot to pick it up as I come out!'

Buster and me drove back, by which time twenty minutes to half an hour had gone by. When we pulled up, there was a window cleaner at the front and right outside the shop was a fucking newspaper stand!

'Front it up, front it up!'

It had a Yale on it, as well as a dirty mortise lock, so we put a screwdriver in and knocked that off. Buster brings the radiogram out and puts it in the boot of the Zephyr, down the next street. But they've seen Buster and me. We catch up down a lay-by.

'We've got it.'

'Oh, thank God for that!'

I drive back to London and I've got three lock-up garages I'm renting down Herne Hill.

I had loads of bent gear in there – it was like a wholesale place, loads of LP records too. I had one of those little silver-grey Ford 500cwt vans; it was nice for me, and nice for taking the kids out. Tommy comes to me and says, 'I've got a couple of customers.' So we load up and off he goes in my van. But, instead of delivering the stuff, he goes to his father's pitch. And while he's there the Old Bill pounce, nicking them for street bookmaking.

'Whose van's this? What's in it?'

Who's it registered to? *Me!* They've got my van down the nick and I've got to go and get it. But, before I know it, in the morning they're bang-bang-bang on my door. I know they've got two witnesses and I am fucking nicked.

I'm not fully dressed, but down the next street there's a bombsite where I used to leave my car. I go out the back way. They're going, 'Open up, it's the police!' and banging on the door. I've only got my trousers, shoes and shirt on – I never had time to put a jacket on. Maureen's opened the door to them. They've come tearing in. I'm over the back garden to the next street, got to the turning with the car, but they're right on me. I was nicked in the car as they'd surrounded the next street.

I got some bird for that: two years, but in stages. I was in Brixton, but from there I went to the Isle of Sheppey – and then back to Brixton for six weeks on a motoring offence, driving without a licence. Later, I was wanted again for another robbery and I had to leave south London, but this time I got away. It was 1958 and I went to the East End because Charlie Kray used to come over to me. He was working over there with a big buyer, who bought lorry loads of stuff. Charlie was introduced to me and used to buy from my lock-ups.

When I went over there on my toes, I met Charlie and his wife Dolly. They said, 'We've got somewhere you can hole up. Ronnie's got a flat in Adelina Grove,' which is opposite The Blind Beggar. Sidney Street, where Churchill laid siege to 'Peter the Painter' (ringleader of a group of East European anarchists and armed thieves cornered in the East End in 1911), was at the side of it. Those flats are really expensive now; they want a fucking fortune for them. But it was like two rooms – a kitchen, and you went outside to a verandah, where the toilet was.

It wasn't in good nick but I had it all done up in what were modern styles then. There was a gay fella, John, who used to work on the firm for the twins. He was good at fashion and designing and he helped me do it up when I took Maureen over there. It had been a shithole, really. But Jamie (overleaf, with Buster Edwards) went to the local school round the corner. I was under the name of Freddie Puttnam, Maureen's brother's name, so I took his identity and I lived over there for quite a while. That's Ronnie Kray's legs on the right-hand side, when he was on his toes from Epsom mental hospital. It was the first time I'd met him.

I had a nice place over in Herne Hill but I had to let it out to Ronnie King, who was an ABA champion. My Jamie was born in Million Road, Herne Hill; the doctor and the midwives delivered him in the next room. I've actually got a photo somewhere of Jamie just after he's been born.

Charlie had said, 'Come round the house and meet my mother and the twins.' But I wasn't too keen because I knew their reputation: they were always beating people up at that snooker hall they had, and getting into rows and trouble. I was out to make money but they were a lot different, though they were opening up spiels then and getting into long firms.

Eventually I went into one of their spiels. Maureen was sitting in the car outside and she said, 'I saw the police vans come round and they all steamed out. I knew you were nicked.' With all the other guys I was done in Harper Square for illegal gambling.

I was in the cells and they said, 'We're gonna take your

dabs and see if you're wanted.' So I'm thinking, 'Fucking hell, I hope I can pay the fine now and get out of the nick.' So, I'm in the dock and we're getting silly £2 fines, but there were a lot of us. I can see these CID coppers over the side of the court. As I went to walk out, they said, ''Ello, Fred, we've been lookin' for you. What you doin' over 'ere?'

So, they walked me to the car park. There were three of us; then all of a sudden there were four. I look round and there's my George walking at the side of me.

'What you gonna do, Fred?'

He's got a stick down his trousers and he thinks I'm

going to have it away again. But the copper said to me, 'Albert's been round and had a word.' This was Albert Connell, the bookmaker, who was a straightener with the coppers. He wasn't a grass – he was a good man who got people out of lots of trouble. Maureen's been round to see him and he's gone into Carter Street, where they issued the warrants.

So, I know I've got a bit of help and I've said, 'What you doin', George? Fuck off! Go on, everything's all right!'

The coppers have gone, ''Oo the fuckin' 'ell's 'e walkin' along with us?'

He left us and they drove me down to Carter Street. The geezer behind the desk said, 'Do you want me to handle it? You're gonna get a bit of time.'

My hands are tied; you do what you have to do. He phoned up Southampton: 'We've got this guy you've been lookin' for, Freddie Foreman, what d'ya wanna do? It's two years old now – are them witnesses still available? D'ya want me to deal with it or do you want me to send him down to you? I've got him on receiving, not the actual robbery.'

'All right, leave it to me.'

'How's that?' he said to me.

'Yeah, cushty, fine.'

So I went to Wandsworth nick for six months, which was nothing. After that I got to know the twins and Charlie very well. That's how it all started.

When I came out, I moved on and got another firm round me: Alfie Gerard, Ronnie Everett and Mickey Regan. Older, more professional people to work with.

I'd just come out of Wandsworth in the left-hand picture. I put Gregory in a good school when I got my pub, years later: Oakfield College in Dulwich. From there, he and Jamie went to the boarding school up on Blackheath, Christ's College. Gregory said, 'I'll go there if Jamie follows me when he's old enough.' He'd got caught up on London Bridge with some other kids, nicking stuff off the backs of lorries, and there were no decent schools at the Elephant & Castle. I had the house at Dulwich Village – ten grand for a house there in the sixties. So I gave them the best education at the time. They've had no convictions and never had any trouble – they've never needed to, they've had a good life.

We've got the three kids in the second photo. Jamie (left) came along about six years after Gregory, and Danielle (right) another three years later.

There's Buster Edwards in Cornwall with his wife June (seated), with my boys and Maureen. June was pregnant with a little girl, her first baby, but the baby died. I took the photo.

That's my second firm there, with our wives at a boxing dinner at the Dorchester in the very early 1960s. The only ones missing are Alf Gerard and Mickey Regan; Alf wasn't photographed very often. There's Ronnie Everett (tall guy on the right); 'Dingdong Del' Rudell (second from right), once a bookmaker in the gambling business; Lenny

White (in glasses), who used to work with me when I was doing the shops; and Johnny Mason (second from left), who came on the firm with Mickey and me.

This is Alfie Gerard and his son Nicky. People were petrified of Alf – he could be terrifying, but he had a heart of gold. He was such a lovely guy, but he wouldn't suffer fools gladly. Things were black and white with him, there was no grey; you either accepted people or you didn't, that was his style. But he was solid, loyal as they come.

Alf died in Brighton in 1981; he had food poisoning. Jerry Callaghan, another member of the Foreman firm, was with him and should have taken him to hospital – his stomach was swelling up and he was ill. He died in the fucking

lift going to the surgery; he should have been taken earlier, but they were on their toes as usual. That's why he didn't want to surface. Mind you, Alf was a terrible eater – he'd eat six pies and mash at once.

Alf had a fish restaurant in Bermondsey called The Blue Plaice. He came out of the back one day when I went down with Maureen before they opened. I said I fancied some eels and he called out to his chef, 'Scatty Eddie' Watkins, who would later shoot a customs officer in 1979. He gave him a job because Eddie used to cook for him in the nick. Alf comes out with his white outfit on. He's got a big knife in one hand and a huge conger eel with its head hanging off, covered in blood down the front where he's been having a carve-up.

Maureen nearly threw up: 'Let's go and have some Italian!'

'What's the fuckin' matter with 'er?' he said.

'See ya later, Alf!'

His little boy was Gregory's age, so they were friendly and grew up together. It was tragic what happened to young Nicky – but of course Nicky turned into a fucking villain, like his dad.

In 1970 he killed Tony Zomparelli in a Soho arcade. Ronnie Knight (married at the time to the actress Barbara Windsor) was accused of giving him the money to do it, because Zomparelli had stabbed his brother David to death in a West End club, but he was later acquitted.

Then Nicky had trouble with Tommy Hole Senior and Junior, some nonsense over his wife. He went out to get some booze for his kid's birthday party in 1982, then they plotted up and shot him. He got out of the car but they were hitting him over the head with the shotguns. They made a right messy job of it.

Years later, they were both paid back. Young Tommy Hole hanged himself in Parkhurst in 1991, then in 1999 the old man was shot at the Beckton Arms in Canning Town.

That's Big Georgie Cahill on the left – he had a scrap-metal yard. One of the firm, he was good at the old fizzer (burning open safes) because he could use a torch and cut up metal.

This is Scotch Pat Connolly (left), and Henry Cooper, in 1961; Red-Faced Tommy (second from left) – 'The Jar', they used to call him – would sell zircon rings with snide

diamonds to publicans' wives and got a lot of money out of it; that's Henry Cooper, obviously; Bert 'Battles' Rossi (right), the Italian was convicted of the slashing of Jack Spot (Jewish East End gangland leader in the pre-Krays era) in 1956, alongside Teddy Dennis, Bill Blythe, Bobby Warren and Mad Frankie Fraser. Dennis and Blythe did the cutting.

That was when the Krays opened the gym at the Double R club. I took Buster, Ronnie King and Tommy McGovern with me. I worked with Tommy when I was on the meat market; I used to pick him up at three in the morning. That's Sulky Gower on the right, manager of the Astor Club; next to him, Jim Wicks, the manager of Henry Cooper, me, Reggie Kray, Red-Face, Charlie and Ron Kray. We used to go down the Astor after all the boxing matches, from all the different parts of London; the twins were the East End and I was south London – they used to call it 'Indian country', coming over to the fucking south! They came firm-handed when they came to my pub, The Prince of Wales. The Astor was neutral territory, where we could all go.

In front at the ringside (Page 40) are Tim Riley, editor of *Boxing News*, and Charlie Kray Senior (second left and centre). Next to me at the back is Buller Ward (top left), whom Reggie Kray ended up slashing because he was minding Tony Maffia. Buller wouldn't let them in on the action so they did him in the Regency Club – Reggie was a fucking liberty-taker, but a good man.

When I look back over it, I realise I never really liked him as a person. I didn't trust him. Ronnie was definitely the nuttiest, because he had mental breakdowns, but he was on tranquillisers that would knock a horse over. He used to give them sometimes to people on his firm and they were out for two days. He'd giggle about it – *hee-hee-hee!* I liked Ronnie, but I always felt Reggie sat on the fence and would go whatever way suited him.

I once had a little fallout upstairs in their house with the Nash brothers (Islington-born-and-bred family firm, whose reputation predated that of the Krays, with whom they shared a cautious respect). It could have got nasty because I was on my own and he had his brothers there – Roy, Billy John, George and Jimmy, who was the more dangerous of them. 'It's gonna go off 'ere, they are gonna have a go at me,' I thought. It was only Ronnie Kray and Jimmy Nash who talked sense and calmed the situation down. Reggie never took my side. I thought, 'You ain't said a word, you would've let it happen. If Ronnie hadn't have been there they'd have set about me.' And that would have been a big mistake.

But Ronnie was all right, and so was Jimmy – it turned out that I saved Jimmy Nash and Joey Pyle from getting topped for the Pen Club shooting, in 1960 (in Duval Street, off Spitalfields Market; the club's name alluded to its funding by a robbery at the Parker Pen factory). It was Jimmy who actually shot the barman, Selwyn Cooney. At the time, the club was being run by Jerry Callaghan and Billy Ambrose, who were on my firm – they were at the 'Battle of Bow' with me the next year; we were close. In fact, I later saved both of them from being arrested.

I had a meet with the twins and Bill at the Krays' house in Vallance Road, Bethnal Green. Jimmy Nash was charged with the murder of Cooney, as was Joey Pyle from south London. We sat down and said, 'Let's work this out. Who's the main witness for the Prosecution?' Bill had been shot in the stomach as well that day, but he'd said nothing. But Fay Sadler – 'the Kiss of Death', who'd had three boyfriends who all died – was having it with Cooney. One of the witnesses was pregnant – we got her over to Ireland, got her to change her story. All the other witnesses rewrote their statements so they couldn't identify anyone who actually fired a shot.

Jimmy Nash was making little cotton nooses with Joey Pyle when they were in HM Prison, Brixton. He was a little nutty, but, if they'd been found guilty they'd have been topped, no question about it. But the judge said, 'Well, it looks like Mr Cooney stepped in the way of a passing bullet.' They all walked out.

Fucking amazing!

Then there's Albert Donoghue (top, fourth from left), who'd be chief prosecution witness in the Frank Mitchell case; he rolled over. And that's 'The Duke', Dukie Osbourne, next to him on the right, who was later wanted over the shooting of a customs guy in 1979.

When his partner Scatty Eddie Watkins's lorry full of cannabis was surrounded by customs, they phoned me to either find them a safe house or alternatively to help them to cut the puff that they had hidden out of the floors and walls of the container they had. I therefore got myself involved in a very bad situation – one which went terribly wrong for everyone involved. Especially the poor customs officer who was shot dead by Scatty Eddie.

Dukie committed suicide in a flat on Hackney Marshes shortly after; they laid him out on a football pitch. I'd had a passport  made for him to come to America with me. He had a moustache; suited and booted, looked like a military guy – because he went a bit hippie after this photo, mixing with all the drugs crowd. Christine Keeler and all the titled people were puffing away, everyone was at it, but I've never smoked in my life. Dukie had done a twelve-stretch in prison before he killed himself; couldn't face going back.

Most of these people above were on the Kray firm. The two barmen at the Double R club were Cliffy Anderson and John Doyland, the gay fella who did up my flat for me. I nicked the pair of them off the twins when I had The Prince of Wales at Lant Street in the Borough – the street where Charles Dickens lived when his father was in the Marshalsea debtors' prison. I had the lock off Dickens's door in a frame on the pub wall, but that went missing somehow. John and Cliff were well pleased to come and work with me. The twins didn't like it, but I wasn't worried about them. They were the two best barmen they had, really fucking good at their job.

This is Jerry Callaghan (right), who was at the Pen Club shooting; he was one of my firm.

I was a professional thief, but Ronnie and Reggie never nicked a car – they didn't even know how to drive a fucking car! They were using strong-arm to get into clubs and pubs; they were into protection money. Then they got into the long firm – when they'd build up the credit, run out the back door and sell it all. But they were also doing some business with Eddie Pucci (below second from left – with the twins and Charlie Kray), who came over as Frank Sinatra Junior's Mafia minder when he appeared at the Rainbow Rooms in 1963. Pucci was later shot dead on a golf course in Chicago by the Mafia.

Charlie and me used to go high-society gambling with Billy Hill (the nearest thing in London to a godfather figure in the late forties and fifties). He had these chemin-de-fer

clubs for lords and ladies in Knightsbridge and Kensington. They were all illegal, but they used to set them up – you never knew the address where it was going to be held till the last minute. They'd have a buffet table laid out with smoked salmon and all that gear. Charlie and me were there as minders every couple of weeks and we'd go home with a couple of hundred quid – terrific! Red-Faced Tommy used to come in with a deck of cards. Billy Hill and Gypsy, his wife, used to read the cards from his crooked set. They cleaned up with the lords and ladies.

I was there when the twins bought a gambling club in Knightsbridge, Esmeralda's Barn, for two grand. Stefan De Faye was running the booze behind the bar and he used to give me all the drink he got hold of when he was working at this big hotel. All the high rollers used to go there and he would put it on their bill – all these bottles of wine and cigars, they were his little earner when their bill went in. He used to come over with cases of Scotch and Camus brandy; he was educating me in all the different German wines, the Niersteiners and Mosels and that. Stefan was a lovely man; he used to do the *Café Continental* TV programme: 'Welcome to the Café Continental!' It was all juggling and tightrope acts, and cabaret. Word was that the little French singer on there was fucking a very well-known person in the highest government circles!

My mate Mickey Regan (overleaf left, with his wife Chrissie) died in Brighton a few years ago, bless him. He was from a very respected family; the Regans were rivals

to the Nashes – they were even born in the same fucking square in Islington. Their fathers knew each other, but Mick had a bit of a falling-out with the Nashes. I went over and gave him some support. Mick was a good businessman; he had an SP (bookmaker's) office at the Angel over the ChiChi Club. Mick's brother Larry worked for him and his cousin Danny Regan, who was a face.

That's Ronnie Knight with Barbara Windsor in the middle; he was partners with Mick in the A&R Club and I got on well with him. Barbara was lovely; I knew her through the twins and I was at the 1963 premiere of her film, *Sparrows Can't Sing*. Charlie Kray was going with her for a while.

We had a great club down Lambeth Walk in the early

sixties, the Walk-In. I put the money up; Buster Edwards was running the bar; my George was manager; I was behind-the-scenes minder – making sure none of the fucking mugs took liberties, or took over the club as they used to in those days. I put Ronnie King on the door, the ex-fighter I always had on a job – I had him up in my casino as well, on security. He was very well spoken and well behaved.

My sister-in-law Nellie was the barmaid. We had Jock the piano player, Bertie Blake singing, Roaring Twenties dress-up nights. It was successful; we had people coming from all over London. We kept it on time, because Kennington nick was right on top of us.

It was in old warehouse-type premises. You entered via a shopfront before it went long and narrow. We had two floors upstairs, where there was a little SP going on, a bookmaking game. Joe Carter, an ex-lightweight out of Mitcham, was running that. It was like a family-run business, in a way.

Then I get a visit from the local police to tell me there've been some complaints about people leaving of a night, making a noise, slamming car doors – you know how people can be when they're drunk. The copper was Frank Williams.

'Have a drink, Frank.'

We had a chat. He was a commando during the war, captured prisoners and brought them back across the channel. There's a photo of him carrying the British flag at Montecassino. I got on well with him. There was a kind of understanding – he never asked questions about anyone or anything. But it was coming to an end. He told me, 'They want to object to the licence when it comes up.' The club had a short lifespan.

We knew we were going to lose the Walk-In club and we wanted to get insurance money out of it. We couldn't burn the fucking place down – it was all concrete and solid. But my relation was an insurance assessor, so I got him down: 'How can I make a bit of money out of it when we shut up shop?'

'There's not much you can do about it, is there, Fred?'

No, there was nothing we could claim for. But one night Buster had an accident. He'd been drinking; he smashed the car and cut his head. He came on foot, covered in blood.

We'd had enough of it, so we smashed the bloody club up – smashed the whole bar, the mirrors, the jukebox. Buster was shaking his head and spraying blood up the walls, over the furniture. We made out there was a disturbance and a fight, and claimed damages and loss of earnings till the club got fixed. We got out with a few quid, but that was the end of the club.

That's how I got to know Frank Williams. He went from there to the Flying Squad – 'the Sweeney'. Frank was in touch with Albert Connell, the bookmaker, and all those people, so he could put feelers out if I was in trouble. Then it finished up that Jimmy Hussey and Gordon Goody got involved with Buster, and it led to the Great Train Robbery.

Before that, we had a go at a Lloyds Bank van in Bow, in December 1961. It was one that got away. Two guys reversed a flat-back lorry into the bank van – one of those little V8 vans with a reinforced back axle. They didn't expect that at all. Then we came up the side of the van with another lorry that had a tarpaulin sheet where we'd cut out the side of it. We put a hook and chain through the doors and windows and drove off. The doors fell open in midair and exposed the money from the tellers in those big, red-leather cricket bags. They were all lined up, full of cash, from the power companies. It would have been a good bit of work. But there was a City copper, Ted Buckle, and his dog Flash, who jumped out onto the street.

One of our firm was shot through the head. Two guards shot through the windows, but we had no guns; *they* had the shooters. An MP later got up in Parliament and asked how many of these vans were driving round London with armed guards.

'Is this New York or Chicago?'

(It turned out that the two guards from Coutts, the Queen's bank, went for target practice every week.)

When the chain went, Mickey Regan put his arm in and they shot him too. The bullet went through his arm but he still hooked up the van. When we pulled it forward the two doors fell right off. Alf Gerard and I tried to climb in the back but, once they started shooting, one of our firm was crawling on his hands and knees with a bullet wound that went into his head at the base of the skull and out the other side.

'Are we all 'ere?'

'No, where's Bill and Jerry?'

We looked down the side of the bank van to our long-backed lorry. Twenty-five yards further down there's Billy Ambrose and Jerry Callaghan fighting with the copper.

Jerry's swinging on his arm and Bill's got the dog hanging on his arsehole. The three of them were fighting in the road.

I grabbed a stick and jumped out the van. The guards in the back said, 'They're coming back! They're coming back!' and started shooting again.

It's funny how you do things in the heat of the moment. I

ran down the side of the van. They're further down the road now, the three of them struggling and spinning around, the dog still hanging on his arse. I've whacked the dog and he's legged it. I said to the copper, 'Let 'em go!' He's got one under his arm – he was a big, strong bastard, you've got to give him credit. He's got hold of another stick and Jerry's swinging on it.

'You bastard! You bastard!' the copper's saying to me.

'Let 'em fuckin' *go*!'

*Whack!* I gave him another and another. He let them go. Now they were all getting excited in the van again because they thought we were coming back again.

The bullet had entered my friend's ear, ricocheted around the base of his skull and come out the other side. He was nearly brown bread (rhyming slang: brown bread = dead; hence the soubriquet 'Brown Bread Fred', i.e. mess with Fred and you're dead). He had searing red-hot lead tearing through his head and they thought he might get meningitis, so the old doctor pumped him up with antibiotics and drained the wound through the night, then got him to King's College Hospital on Denmark Hill. They had a theatre for brain operations. Maureen, my wife, was up with him all night – he had a bit of a bad turn, not so much from the injury as because he could have got plenty of bird just for being on the scene. But he's about today. He survived to enjoy his life ever since.

There was a big scream about the Battle of Bow: 150 grand on board. It was a big one for that time. We'd have got the prize if not for the guns used by the bank tellers.

Just before the Train Robbery, in May 1963, I robbed forty bars of gold. I buried them in the country. I was going to leave that for a year before I surfaced, because I had the pub and all the coppers were going down the cellar: 'Got any gold bars down 'ere, Fred?'

People were coming to me: 'Oh, Fred, I can buy that gold! Can you come and give me a bit of credibility?'

'Yeah, sure, I'll come with you.' I know it's bollocks because I'm the one who's got it put down. I'm not walking round, going, 'Who wants to buy this?'

There was only one bar that went out on the market, and that was because Tommy my mate had no money. He was brought on the firm because Alf and Ronnie were in the nick; Mick and Big George had gone into business together and were giving it a rest, so I had to make up the firm.

Tommy sold his one bar to a man named Tony Maffia. He was murdered by a man named Jewell, from up north. Maffia was a buyer of tom. He got him out in the car on a moody one of selling some jewellery – 'Bring some money with ya' – and shot him in the head to nick the money off him. He was charged with the murder. When they went to investigate Tony Maffia, they found a safety deposit box and, lo and behold, there's a bar of gold. I never even knew who Tommy had sold it to. He said he wasn't going to market it, so there was no danger of it coming on top, but that was the only one they got back.

This gold was so hot we had to put it down. Every fucking grass in London was trying to find out who'd got it and who was trying to sell it, and some of the frummers in Hatton

# Evening Standard

CITY PRICES

FRIDAY, MAY 24, 1963

WEST END FINAL CLOSING PRICES

## Silent masked robbers make a lightning swoop on treasure from Rothschilds

# £250,000 LONDON BULLION RAID

## Gang flee in van with 40 gold bars

*Evening Standard Reporter*

Forty bars of gold worth between £250,000 and £280,000 were stolen today by a three-man gang in a lightning raid on the bullion broking firm of Sharps Pixley and Co. in Paul Street, Finsbury.

The raiders, in overalls and with nylon stockings over their faces, are believed to have slipped into the firm's warehouse as a bullion delivery van arrived from Rothschild's.

They hid an 80 bars of gold, each weighing 27lb., were unloaded and the van backed out again.

### THEN THEY STRUCK.

Fifty-five-year-old ex-policeman Mr. Percy Houghton, on guard duty by himself, saw the men leaping at him. He was beaten about the head and trussed up.

### INTO A VAN

The raiders, working in silence and at great speed, snatched up all of the gold bars and put them into their own van—a blue Ford similar to the type used by security organisations.

They made their getaway north towards Old Street.

The getaway is believed to have been seen by a worker at a nearby building site.

"I heard a bit of a commotion and then saw two men running out on to the road from the direction of the warehouse," said 21-year-old Bryan Hunt, of Inglewood Road, West Hampstead.

"One of them was big and dark and had something stuffed into his pocket which looked like a policeman's truncheon. The other was smaller and had a slipped-up jacket.

"They jumped into a dark blue van which was moving off and it drove rapidly away."

### A CRY FOR HELP

A few minutes later—at 12.25 p.m.—cries for help were heard by people in a garage opposite the warehouse.

Mr. Arthur Nash, a maintenance engineer, at Walthamstow, ran across to the gates of the warehouse, which were locked.

"I heard shouts of 'Help, Help, I've been robbed,'" said Mr. Nash. "I couldn't get in so I went back and dialled 999."

### BIG SEARCH STARTS

Police under Detective-Superintendent Eric Reid and Detective Chief-Inspector Ian Forbes arrived to find Mr. Houghton, a married man with two daughters, tied in a wicker chair in the yard. He was taken to hospital with facial injuries.

Immediately a big search began in Central and East London for the raiders. Scores of police questioned the people living and working near the warehouse.

*Continued on Back Page, Col. One*

PAUL STREET

### Mac's son-in-law for Moscow

*By PHILIP MARSHALL*

### Bebe Daniels 'unchanged'

WEATHER—Rather warm. See Page 17

Garden were working with the Old Bill. You couldn't trust some of the bastards.

I wanted to get it out of the country and get the right price for it, because each bar had its own quality with the South African rand stamp on it. You couldn't damage it, you had to keep it how it was, because otherwise they'd have it assayed to see if it was pure gold or not – whereas this marking told you it was.

So, I couldn't risk what we had put down and go and get nicked on something else – there was a lot of fucking money there. It was the biggest gold robbery since Captain Blood sailed the Spanish Main – that's what they put in the papers! After a while I got it out to Switzerland. Someone bought me out in Swiss francs and I put them in a Swiss bank account. That's how it was sold, one bar at a time. I was in Geneva for months.

(Later I'm in Brixton, nicked, and I'm in a cell next to this fucking geezer called Jewell. He was the one who shot Tony Maffia and got life for it.)

**FRANK KURYLO:** I was in Cockney Joe Freeman's office one afternoon in Mayfair, and Freddie came in because he knew him. Freddie had about four offices; this was after the Train Robbery. He didn't notice me.

Joe said, 'That fella who was just here, do you know who he is?'

I didn't know his second name, so I said, 'Yeah, it's Freddie from Dulwich.'

'Do you know what his people are doing?'

'Well, I'm not going round with him . . .'

Cockney Joe treated him like he was his own son. Charlie Kray was Freddie's pal – he didn't meet the twins until after about six or seven months of knowing Charlie. That's how I used to see Freddie about.

I knew he was at it, or rather, we *thought* he was at it, we *thought* we knew what he was doing. I know now, but back then nobody knew.

**FREDDIE:** Later in 1963, Roger Cordrey, who did the signal on the Train Robbery, was arrested with the poor old darts player Bill Boal, who he used to have a drink with. The two of them had seen an advert in the newspaper for garages to let. They went down and put Cordrey's Ford Prefect in there. But in the car he had a couple of holdalls. He pulled out the cash and paid in advance. They were all spending the money, which was reported to the police. It turned out that the woman who owned the garages was the widow of a police officer.

That's how Cordrey and Boal got arrested. When they got him in the police station Roger was wriggling about. They said, 'What's the matter with you?' He said, 'I've got to tell you . . . you'll have to get a doctor. I've got a key up my arse.'

He had an ignition key up there, so they got the doctor in. They take it back to open the motor and find a holdall with thirty grand in it. Then they find more money in the other car.

'Where did you get it from?'

'Oh, I can't tell you that . . .'

They go to his house and find more cash, so he's in deeper shit. Boal had some money in his house too. So, they've got them banged up and the Flying Squad are coming down. They pulled them out the cell, giving them the usual treatment, a hard time right through the night.

'Now, tell us who you got the money off of.'

'A fella called Fred.'

'Where did he give it to ya?'

'At the Brighton races.'

'What's his other name?'

'I can't tell you that, I'll get topped.'

Nice statement. But from then on everything went pear-shaped. He was the first one to get nicked. Then Brian Field's father (the crooked solicitor, who conspired on the Great Train Robbery) threw all the money out into the woods, when it hit the newspapers, but he left a little with his name on it at a hotel he stayed in at one time with his wife.

After the Train Robbery, I did the phone-box business – left fifty grand with ten grand on top for Albert Connell, on a separate little parcel wrapped up. But then Superintendent Tommy Butler got in the car with the person who was meant to be getting the money from the phone box and Detective Constable Frank Williams, so they couldn't go to pick it up.

'We've got to go to arrest Jimmy White,' he said.

'We've got to pick some money up.'

'No, that's all bollocks, that won't be there!'

But Williams and his little firm knew it was good information – there was going to be some money from the Train Robbery.

Tommy Wisbey could have walked at that point but the silly bastard wouldn't stand for it. Tommy had left a thumbprint at Leatherslade Farm, the Train Robbers' HQ.

'I've got two alibi witnesses.'

One was Jimmy Kensit, Patsy's dad – he was a pickpocket – and the other was a publican in East Street market, near Walworth Road. The Old Bill went to see them and they rolled over straightaway, said they were approached to give a false alibi.

If Wisbey could have pulled out thirty grand he might have walked from a thirty-year sentence. I'll never forgive him for that. I was close to him and his family.

'I'm trying to get you out of trouble 'ere,' I said.

I was trying to talk to him in a lift, knowing there were probably cameras on me.

'I'll take me chances!' he told me.

'Take your chances? You're going to get a load of bird. What's the matter with you?'

I tried to impress his situation upon him but he wouldn't have it, so he got his thirty years. I was just trying to help him out.

There was nowhere else to drink in those times when the pubs closed halfway through the day. If you went over to Ludgate Circus you could drink for another half-hour. People used to drive over the bridge just for that when they had the flavour.

So, there's a gap here, we've got to do something about this. There were derelict buildings that were going to be pulled down and empty shops waiting for their leases to run out before they demolished them. We got a couple of those places, knocked the wall down in between and made more room, put a bar in the corner and made a 'Shush club' – after the Schweppes advert when they used to go, 'Shh . . .'

Everyone used to come over when the pubs closed at lunchtime, had a drink and went back to the pubs in the evening if they wanted to be out all day; it filled the day. But they often didn't leave our Shush club because they enjoyed themselves so much – we used to have singers, music, dancing. It was like a speakeasy. We named it after the Humphrey Bogart film *Casablanca*. As we closed one down or it got raided, we'd open up somewhere else, where the demolition people were pulling houses down. Hence the club got called Casablanca 1, 2, 3 . . .

'You've gotta get out now,' they'd say, 'we gotta pull the fucking house down! We're holding it up as best we can . . .'

They'd come in and pull the floorboards up; people would just tread over the nails and the gaps. They were jumping over fucking trenches to get into the house! Women were pulling up their skirts between their legs to jump over. We'd say, 'We've still got a lot of stock to sell, you'll have to give us another week.'

We had one in a transport yard with charabancs, in Peckham. The coachmaster would say, 'Now, look, if we get raided then the coach has broken down. We'd got all the booze on board so the twenty-five, thirty people are havin' a drink in 'ere instead of goin' down to Southend. It's their day out, but it's been ruined.'

On the day we did get raided, he was standing there, pissed.

'Give 'em the fuckin' spiel for fuck's sake!'

But he was too drunk to say anything.

They nicked all the booze – the cossers used to take it all back to the station and have a piss-up. But it wasn't that serious a deal, you were just drinking out of hours.

The Shush clubs ran for a long time – all the way up until when they legalised drinking through the day. They were great little places and there was not one bit of trouble in any of them – but, then again, they knew they were mine and George's. What I didn't know was that George had been having an affair with Pat, one of six girls who used to come in on Friday nights. I never knew anything about it, but my sister-in-law Nellie sussed it out and told Maureen. George was going away a bit early when I was closing up; he'd do the till and disappear.

Then all of a sudden, in December 1964, I get a message from one of his daughters that George is in St Thomas's Hospital and he's been shot.

I go up to the hospital and there's coppers everywhere. When I said I was there to see my brother, they said they might have to take his leg off from the hip because it had hit the femoral artery, just past the groin. They had to stop the bleeding and you could have put a bottle in the wound, it was that big. It had been done close up. He was in a bad way, his eyes were sunk in his head; there were big, dark rings and he looked fucking terrible.

They left us alone and I whispered to him, 'Give me a name, George.'

He whispered, 'Ginger Tom.'

When George was having a meal with his wife and kids, he'd heard a knock at the door and gone to answer it. There was this guy standing there, asking for a fictitious person. George said, 'I don't know anyone of that name.'

'Oh, okay, mate.'

He shut the door but he thought, 'I recognise him, I know him from somewhere.'

I pieced it together. There was a bloke running car sites at the time who fitted the bill. 'Yeah, that's him. That's Ginger Tom – Tommy Marks,' I thought.

Of course the twins knew him: 'Yeah, Ginger Marks goes round with that fuckin' Jimmy Evans, he runs with him.'

Charlie said, 'They're goin' on a bit of work Saturday night and they want me to handle the tom from it. They're doin' the jeweller's round in Bethnal Green Road.'

Right away, I've put it together: I've got names, and it was Evans's bird that George was getting hold of. He was a face – he used to burn warehouses down for the Jewish mob and things like that. Apart from that, I'd never met him or seen him before. But now Charlie's talking to them about their bent gear: 'Don't take it to no one else, bring it to me and I'll give you a good deal.' They said they'd bring it round straight after they'd done Attenborough's, the jeweller's.

I was told that on that Saturday, as luck would have it, a car door opened, Marks and Evans came out two-handed and started walking towards Bethnal Green Road. The people who were on their case and keeping watch on their

# POLICE PROBE MURDER WITHOUT A BODY

### By CHARLES SANDELL

AT two police stations in the East End of London last night the lights were burning late as Det. Supt. Ron Townsend and a team of detectives worked on the mystery of the murder without a body.

And as the pubs began to hum in the heart of Cockneyland the talk in many of them was about Ginger Marks.

For it was last Saturday night that Thomas Albert (Ginger) Marks stepped out of his home in Redman's-road, Stepney, and into danger. And after a gun battle a mile away Ginger disappeared.

Marks, aged 37, a car salesman and haulier, was dressed in a green tweed suit and a light check mackintosh.

Ginger, the man everybody knew, stepped out every Saturday night, usually with his wife Anne, who is expecting her third baby in four months' time.

But last Saturday Ginger went out alone, and he didn't go to any of his usual haunts.

He had been quiet and subdued since he received a threatening phone call just before Christmas. And that night he walked straight past one of his favourite locals, The Rose and Punch Bowl.

### Scream

Then, just after midnight, shots rang out in Cheshire-street, a half-mile away from Redman's-road.

Then there was a scream and the roar of a car getting away in a hurry.

An hour later as Anne Marks answered the phone a cold voice said: "Your husband has been shot and taken off in a car." Then the line went dead.

But in Cheshire-street the police found few traces of the shooting.

After a dawn search they turned up a spent .22 cartridge, a bloodstain on the pavement, and what could have been a bullet hole in the wall.

They believe someone had been shot in the stomach at close range, and the bullet had gone through him into the wall. They are treating their inquiry as a murder investigation.

But no hospital treated a wounded man, no waste ground or river has yielded a body so far. There is still no proof that there has even been a murder.

### Shut up

Searching detectives found that suddenly the East End had shut up. Nobody knew anything.

I spoke to Ginger's old friend, Patsie Quill, who keeps The Blind Beggar, in the Mile End-road.

He said: "Everybody knew Ginger. He had a way of laughing loudly so that anybody who didn't know him would ask who he was.

"I know him as well as anybody and I can't think of an enemy. But you don't know who your enemies are until they, do something to you, do you?"

Ginger did have enemies. Perhaps three strangers reported as having been with him last Saturday night were among them.

So far there have been no real clues to the truth about the murder without a body. But in the pubs East End pubs last night they were waiting for something big to happen.

---

# Where is Ginger Marks?

### WE OFFER £5,000 REWARD FOR HIM—DEAD OR ALIVE

*NEWS OF THE WORLD REPORTER*

TODAY the News of the World offers a reward of £5,000 for information that leads to the discovery, dead or alive, of Ginger Marks. Marks is the man who vanished a fortnight ago after a shooting incident in London's East End.

His disappearance has now become one of the greatest underworld mysteries of modern times.

Every clue, with Marks's broken spectacles, a cartridge case, a bullet hole, and bloodstains in an alley as the only clues, it is becoming deeper and more sinister.

Our reward will be paid, at the Editor's absolute discretion, to the first person who provides information to the police leading directly to the discovery of Ginger Marks, dead or alive.

It will not, of course, be paid to anyone who may be involved in criminal proceedings as a result of the inquiry, and the Editor's judgment on all matters connected with the offer must be accepted as final.

Full of the reward offer last night, his wife Anne, said: "This is wonderful news, I'm sure it will help in clear up the mystery. I'm so terribly worried, but at least I feel I'd get help from the police in finding out about my husband."

### Then Mrs Marks made a dramatic appeal

"Romantic must know what has happened," she said. "Please, whoever you are, tell me if my husband is alive or dead. I beg you to put me out of this agony of not knowing."

### Guarded

Police have guarded Mrs Marks day and night in her flat at Redman's-road, Stepney, since the shooting. She has refused to see anyone, but returns to one thought:

But last night all she made her appeal through the News of the World, she tried to be cautiously, her aide at the door of her flat said: Collyer Marks.

All that was known to Mrs Marks is that Ginger stepped out alone on a Saturday night at 11.30 p.m. people in Cheshire-street. Near Cheshire-street, close together, the sound of rushing of guns. A man screams, the sound of gunfire and a car being driven off at speed.

### Guarded

Half an hour later, Mrs Marks received a mysterious phone call telling her that her husband had been shot.

Apart from the clues Marks by the police in the alley where nothing no body was found.

The area was seething with rumours, and an intimate police hunt, led by Chief Det Insp. Ron Townsend has done no discernible.

But there is still no sign of the missing man.

### I waited

Last night Mrs. Marks told me of the last time she saw her husband.

"I am I always left him that night, Ginger and I went out because she always went out together. We had our favourite pubs in the East End, and had friends in every one of them.

"On the Friday before Tom disappeared I'd a feeling something was wrong. We didn't go out that night.

Tom asked how I felt the next night and when I said I'd looked at it I gave it. I thought if he looked out of sorts and felt a while I said it was all right.

"He wasn't dressed to go anywhere much. He wore a greasy tweed jacket, matching greenish trousers, and a navy blue gaberdine raincoat.

"I sat up waiting for him. I thought he'd got mixed up in some unexpected party, but he never made much of his midnight. I started to get a bit fluttery.

Then I got this phone call. 'Your husband's been shot,' he's had it, it was all that was said. I couldn't believe it. I thought it was a joke.

"But at two o'clock I slipped on my coat and...

---

**GINGER MARKS**
Missing, believed shot

knocked up Tom's brother round the corner. He said we'd better go to the police.

"At 4 o'clock some police-station they checked all the details and put out a search for Tom."

Then Mrs Marks went home through of a shooting in Cheshire-street and, of course, I could identify Tom's spectacles."

Fresh as a herald a few days after Marks's disappearance, a stranger called at Beulah-hill, South Norwood Surrey.

### This was the 'House of Records,' so-called because there were peculiar roaming the streets.

There was no one in the house and the police found nothing that could lead them to Ginger Marks.

According to the electoral roll, the house of the home of Mr. James Evans and Mrs. Marks if she knew him.

"Yes," she said, "he's a business friend of Tom's. I think they did some transport deals together.

One theory, passed on to police from underworld sources, is that Marks was the unwilling victim of a crime of passion.

### Vengeance

About six weeks ago detectives were told a Kennington man who had been having an affair with a gangster's wife was shot between the two.

A second story is that the man would vengeance on the gang who shot the shooting by shot and Marks have been married. They have two children, Barbara, aged 14, and Michael, 10, and she esteems another child in May.

"My wife always des devotedly in love," she said. "He was always so kind and serious making out that Tom was a dependable villain. All night nearly say he had trouble with the law. But he's been finished with all that for a long time.

"He has always been in cars and run some sort of transport business all his life. Car business now. But he's never gone though peculiar since I can't understand how he came to be shot and can't understand why anybody could be cruel enough to leave me in torment like this."

movements followed them at a distance, tailed them down the back, near a church. The rest of the firm was already in the jeweller's, two-handed inside. They had already been in there, apparently, and had come out. It was fate, really.

When they got to where the Repton Club was, just past The Carpenter's Arms (the Kray twins' local), one of the street lights was out. That's where Marks was done. Evans ran round the street and hung underneath a lorry, got his legs up and held on.

Evans went home to his wife, Pat, and said, 'You nearly got me fuckin' killed tonight!' He was putting his fingers through the bullet holes in his coat because he'd held Marks up as a shield.

'Who was it?' she asked him.

'I don't know who the fuck it was! It was too dark there, I couldn't see!'

That was as far as it went at the time.

Years later, when we were interviewed by the police, George had carried on his relationship with Pat for twelve years or so. All she had to do was tell the truth: Evans had come home, put his finger through the bullet holes in his coat and said he didn't know who had done it. It was too dark and it happened too quickly, he couldn't identify anybody. Evans didn't know – he would have said so if he did.

But would she do it? She wouldn't make a statement because she was frightened of this fucking Evans (below, pointing to a bullet hole near Attenborough's jeweller's). He used to batter her and beat her up, and lock her in. He was

**NEWS** OF THE **WORLD**

SUNDAY, APRIL 11, 1965    EMPIRE NEWS    No. 6,335    PRICE SIXPENCE

# I SAW GINGER MARKS SHOT

## Man who fled as guns blazed tells of 'a cold blooded murder'

### By George Evans

HIRED killers shot Tommy "Ginger" Marks—and spirited away his body. I know. I was there. Just two feet away.

I heard shots and saw my friend Ginger clutch at his chest and stagger back.

Continued on Page 4

a sick, wicked bastard. He'd already cut someone's thumb off because the guy put his hand down when he went for his bollocks. That was someone else he'd accused of having it off with her.

She didn't help one fucking bit. I never spoke to her or had anything much to do with her after that.

It's funny because, when Evans was in the nick in the seventies, he had three witnesses who were after a bit of parole. One made a statement to the effect that Alf Gerard, who was on a different wing, was trying to get someone to poison Evans's food.

Evans was in for stabbing this Scottish kid, who was down in London with his girlfriend. He chased him round his car over a row with his new French wife and stabbed him to death. He was charged with murder but they reduced it to manslaughter after he said, 'I'll tell you who was in the car that night' on the Ginger Marks case. So he rolled over and they gave him seven years.

He was up in court to give evidence on two trials that I faced. The judges were the ones who'd just weighed off the Guildford Four for thirty years apiece. The jury just couldn't agree in Court Two, so we went to Court One in front of John Donaldson, who was made Master of the Rolls afterwards.

Two coppers gave evidence but put the wrong date at the top of it – they said 6 January instead of the 8th (which it was), but they'd never interviewed anyone then. They'd written down the answers on the questionnaires – 'Foreman said follow them down this road, don't get too close.' I'm supposedly giving instructions from the back of the car, but they didn't realise they'd dated it on a clean sheet of paper.

We had a great QC, Louis Hawser: 'You conducted the interview, you dated it, you timed it, question and answer . . . Okay, show us your notebook. Please sit down and don't leave the court.'

He called the other copper in so the first one couldn't

mark his card. They'd already given this evidence at the magistrates' court prior to its going to the Old Bailey, so it was previously quoted.

'Just look up into the corner, where you put the date. Can you read it out?'

As soon as he read the date, he realised: they'd made the statements out days before they ever arrested Ronnie Everett, Alf Gerard or Jerry Callaghan. Mine was, 'No comment – no comment – no comment,' but on their statement there was all this 'verbal'. Then they put the wrong fucking date on it! Of course it had to be thrown out.

We're all eating at the Jack of Clubs restaurant here. On the right of this picture (overleaf) is my barmaid from The Prince of Wales, Maggie Furminger. Her husband Terry was my customer, worked in the print.

When Biggsy (Great Train Robber Ronnie Biggs) escaped from Wandsworth in 1965 I looked after him, had him holed up. His wife Charmian was down on the coast. When he was most wanted, I took him down to see her before they split up because they wanted to get out of the country. Maggie got the passport for Charmian and she went out as Maggie Furminger; Biggsy went out as Terry Furminger at a later date.

I got Biggsy out via a boat at London Bridge. Charmian wasn't so recognisable as she wasn't wanted – there weren't any posters up. But Biggsy had to have his face done. I put him on an old tramper going over to Antwerp. I gave Maggie five hundred quid to get the pictures done and get

a passport. Then I got Ronnie King to get Biggsy another passport when he went from Australia.

I went on holiday to Jamaica with the wife and kids. While I was up in the plane, Ronnie Everett, Alfie Gerard and Jerry Callaghan went round to the lock-up I used to have in Herne Hill – we had vans, Post Office uniforms, cutting gear and shotguns. They went there to tune up a Ford Zephyr and the Old Bill walked in on them. Two coppers wanted to look at the cars, and they had a fucking fight. It finished up in the office using chairs and God knows what.

They got away; some women were pulling out of a turning and they pulled them out of the car, nicked it and drove off. A gas gun was fired; it wasn't a real gun, but they were wanted for attempted shooting of the police. The coppers tried to nick me for it, too, but I'd been on my way to Jamaica. My poor old sister-in-law, Nell, was held in the kitchen with an Alsatian dog in her face.

The firm were holed up and I had to get them out to Australia the same way as Biggsy, who'd already been out there for years. They bought houses, had businesses: a trucking business, hardware shops. So they got established.

But then the satellite pictures came over of Biggsy and Eric Flower, a pal of ours who used to come to work with us. Suddenly, they're all on the television and they get nicked out there. Biggsy was the only one who escaped; he got to Brazil. Otherwise he'd have got his thirty years because Paul Seabourn, who helped him escape over the wall into the furniture vehicle, was taken into the nick three times. He knew where he was; he put him in the flat. I said, 'We've got to move him, I don't like it.' They got Seabourn a fourth time, so I went up there and moved Biggsy and Eric to another safe house. It was my own fucking flat I put them in, on the Kennington Estate!

Next thing I know, they've kicked the door in of the flat underneath. It's a bit close to home. I knew Seabourn in Leicester when he was doing a ten-stretch there, so he hadn't been out that long.

The lady on the right (overleaf) is Mary Gorbell. Her husband Bill worked for Tommy Wisbey and myself in the Borough. Mary used to work in the champagne bar at the races, where she was known as 'Marilyn'. Bill Gorbell was a good settler; he settled the bets. Tommy Wisbey was running the front counter. I had other betting shops at Nunhead Lane, Brixton Hill and Croydon Lane. Nosher Powell was minder of this restaurant, the Jack of Clubs, and he did a lot of film work as an extra.

Round the corner from my pub was the Marshalsea, which was a dosshouse. A row of houses had been converted into a prison, back in the seventeenth century, and now all the old dossers had their beds there. It still had the old windows and it's still standing today – you can go and see it. But it had quite a lot of floors in it, so I thought I'd open a gym in there. I had a twenty-three-year lease on it – I took it over and converted the whole building.

Down in the basement, in the mid-sixties, I had recording studios and rehearsal rooms. I had the Small Faces down

there, Cat Stevens, the Spencer Davis Group. My nephew, Eddie Hardin, who went to school with my Gregory, was a natural musician. He wasn't a streetwise kid, but when it came to music he could play anything.

When Steve Winwood left in 1967, Spencer Davis wanted someone to take his place; I took Eddie up on audition and he got the job! He could sing and play keyboards exactly like Winwood; you couldn't tell the difference. I got him to audition for the job down at the old cinema in Barnes, where they did the rehearsals and recording, with Shirley Bassey's arranger. I paid £1,500 for the session, which was a lot of money then. But, when Spencer took him on, the kid made a shitload of money and I never got a penny back!

When the Spencer Davis Group split up in 1968, Eddie and Pete York, the drummer, formed their own band. They were having number-one hits in Germany; he bought a house in Sunningdale with great big columns and top-of-the-range motors. He did all right for himself.

I could have been an impresario. I could spot talent when I saw it, and I could have nurtured it. Crime was only a business. To me, the worst crime was for a man to bring his family up in poverty, but how you get your money is another matter.

My Maureen used to say, 'When you gonna stop this? Why don't you stop now? We've got enough.' But I would say to her, 'It's only business.' I should have listened to her. We had six betting shops and the 211 Club in Balham, which was fucking massive – it's the Polish Embassy today.

It was Lady Hamilton's house, which Nelson bought for her. It had a ballroom at the side of it, where I put a boxing show on – that's how big it was. But the police from Tooting stopped it because the twins came over: 'What's the twins doin' on our patch?'

This is Mark Rowe, a good light middleweight, with Maureen and me at my Chaps gym. Next to him is Phil Lundrigan from the Boxing Board of Control; he was ringside all the time. And of course that's Dave Charnley (right), 'the Dartford Destroyer', who should have been a world champion when he fought Joe Brown for the title.

This is Tim Riley on the right. He was the editor of *Boxing News*; next to him is Ron Oliver, who was a boxing writer; Bill Chevalier (in the ring) was Rowe's trainer; Gordon W. Prange (ringside, second from left) was the author of a book called *Tora! Tora! Tora!*, which they made into a film about Pearl Harbor and made him a shitload of money.

The first time Frank Mitchell (overleaf) got a conviction he'd stolen a bike. But his father never took him round the house and said, 'Give him the bike back' – he took him to the police station and got him nicked. That was the first time he had a brush with the law, so his father didn't do him any favours. I suppose that traumatised him a little bit.

He wasn't a well boy. They certified him and he went to Rampton, the secure hospital in Nottinghamshire. I don't know what they sent him there for, but it must have been serious. He was notorious in prison for attacking screws and prisoners: cutting them, breaking ribs with bear hugs. Frank was immensely strong, but with a twelve-year-old's brain, chucking his toys out the pram.

He was very vicious and stabbed a friend of mine, Bruce Reynolds, mastermind of the Great Train Robbery, in the bathhouse. Bruce kept a lid on that, never wanted to talk about it. Mitchell was charged, but he went to magistrates' court and was found not guilty. I suppose there were no other witnesses, but Bruce was badly attacked.

Ronnie Kray paled Mitchell up when he was doing four years in Wandsworth. Mitchell terrorised the whole nick. The screws were frightened of him; it took a lot to control him. He'd go in the gym and, if someone could lift a certain weight, he'd up it ten times – he had to be the number one at everything.

He'd escaped with a fella from Rampton nuthouse; they were called 'the mad axemen' for terrorising people, breaking into their houses with axes. But they were captured and got the birch for punishment. They couldn't handle Mitchell there so he went to Broadmoor. Fuck me if he doesn't escape again!

He gets himself an axe for the second time and terrorises an old couple – nicks their money, their jewellery, their Ford Fiesta (though I wouldn't have thought he could drive it). He's recaptured and the next time he escapes is from Dartmoor. They let him go down to the village there and he was treating everyone in the pub. He'd apparently been fucking a schoolmistress in a barn there and going to buy budgerigars. They never searched him. He had a charmed life there; the governor was very easy on him. No screws were allowed in his cell, though he had a knife he was going around with.

But in late 1966 the twins told him they'd take him back to London, where they'd campaign for his freedom. Now, he's regarded as the most dangerous criminal to escape. They've got the Army out on the moor with loaded rifles, looking for him – they're going to shoot him on sight. The press are covering him: 'Lock up your women and children, your dogs and cats. Lock up your home. Don't step outside the house.' They've got these cartoons of him under bridges like a fucking big ape or monster.

And of course he's still got the knife on him – he showed it to Albert Donoghue, who threw it away with his clothing on the way back from the Moor. They take him into this house with Billy Exley and Scotch Jack Dickson as minders. They were sleeping all over the place since there was only one bedroom: on the floor, on the settee. He was kicking off all the time – he was going over to see the twins' mother, or his own mother. They sent out for some fish and chips; they never got him a saveloy, so he fucking kicks off again. He's got to win every game of cards. He's doing press-ups and chinning the bar; he's picking them up by their belts above his head.

And now he wants to go out and get himself a bird. So they get him a hostess and he's fucking the life out of her. She's only supposed to be there one night but becomes a prisoner – for twelve days altogether. When she tried to escape out the window, he caught her and pulled her back in.

He's cleaning his teeth every five fucking minutes, all this weird behaviour. He's picking up this iron-framed piano on his own to show how strong he is. Reggie Kray once went to see him and he got him arm wrestling – and of course he won every time. He's a strong bastard. But now Exley is saying, 'I'm not looking after this cunt – he's got a fucking tool!' He's got a shooter on him.

Exley's woken one morning by being tickled under the chin, and he's looking down the barrel of his own fucking gun. Mitchell has gone down his pockets and found the shooter – none of which the twins or anybody else mentioned to me. He's carrying one of the kitchen knives as well and has sworn to take six coppers with him rather than go back to prison, because he'll never get out after this.

'I want to live out in the country with Ronnie,' he says, because Ronnie has bullshitted him: 'No one will know you there.' Like *Of Mice and Men*: 'Tell me about the rabbits, George.' He's in this dreamworld and thinks he's going to get away with it. No way is he going to give himself up – there are six bullets in the gun. So, he's become a complete liability. They've come to me to ask what I can do to help them. Like a fucking idiot, I stood for it.

When I've come to take him down to the country, to see what can be done with him, as he comes out of the door with Albert there's a fucking copper walking towards him. Mitchell panicked. As Albert said in his book *The Enforcer*, he had to calm him down: 'He won't recognise you – he'll recognise *me*.' The copper just kept on walking, took no notice. He was lucky that he never said, 'Excuse me, sir . . .'

He'd have been a goner.

Mitchell gets in the back of the van and pulls out the fucking shooter! I've got my back to him, talking to Donoghue in the front. He's saying, 'We want to go through the tunnel – we go straight down 'ere and turn right . . .'

Then all I hear is, 'Look what I've got!'

Alf Gerard's gone mad. He's sitting on the other side and, Mitchell being the nutty bastard that he is, there's got to be a shootout now.

Right, then, I'll stop there and sling him out.

But he went straight to the back of the fucking van. It wasn't intended for anything to happen there: it was too close to the house we'd just walked out of. It was ridiculous: there were neighbours either side and if they stood on the pavement they could see him get into the back.

When I got to Leicester Prison, the governor came to see me in the cell, with the chief warden and the top brass:

# UNSOLVED, THE RIDDLE OF THE AXEMAN WHO VANISHED

By TOM TULLETT, EDWARD VALE and BRIAN MacCONNELL

FRANK MITCHELL was nearly ten. Like his friends, he dearly wanted a bike. Like his friends, he couldn't have one.

*Frank Mitchell . . . He escaped from Dartmoor, and then he vanished.*

This was Axeman Frank Mitchell's lone nest on Dartmoor . . . the hideaway at lonely Bagga Tor where he brought his drink and his women.

## HE 'RAN DARTMOOR'

## 'Guv'nor' Foreman misses the party at his pub

By DAVID WRIGHT

*Foreman . . still in jail*

'Foreman, if it's true what you did regarding the Mitchell case, you need a medal the size of a dustbin lid.'

That's the fucking governor of the nick!

But they were cunning bastards, the twins. They never told me about him having a gun. They wouldn't go to see him themselves. Ronnie was in hiding because he'd spoken to a copper in the pub and taped it all – who'd wanted twenty-five quid a week for letting him drink in the pub, or some shit. He should never have done that, the silly fella, but he was hiding because he'd never give evidence against *anyone*, even a copper. Which is right.

So, that was the situation and they left me to deal with it – but it was after the work they did with the Marks thing, over George. They'd also put one of our people from the Battle of Bow into Dr Blasker's surgery and cleared him up with an alibi – he might have got a fifteen, you don't know how much bird he'd have got otherwise. So, that was a big favour I owed them for helping my friend out of trouble. I was truly indebted, and they'd looked after me when I'd had it on my toes from south London; they put me in the Colony Club as well. So there were quite a few reasons why I should help them out.

That's Maureen, Ronnie and me with George Raft when I had The Prince of Wales, but that was later on in the 1960s. Like James Cagney, New York-born movie actor

Raft was originally a song-and-dance man before becoming associated with gangster roles – most notably in support to Paul Muni in the original classic film version of *Scarface* (1932). When they brought all the gaming machines over, I was the first customer of the American Gabe Foreman (same name as mine) for the one-armed bandits. They were illegal then, but we put them in all the little cafés and drinkers. Frankie Fraser and Eddie Richardson got into it as well, but we were the first. They were our rivals; they had a place in Wardour Street.

When I opened a casino in the early 1960s, the 211 Club in Balham, George Raft came over for the opening. The Nashes, the twins and I had been drawing money out of George's Colony Club. That was how it worked, like in New York – you had to have the three firms, who all got their bit out of anything.

George was respected as an actor; he'd made loads of films. But that night I asked him: 'Who was the main man who gave you help, George?' He said it was a Yorkshireman, Owney Madden. He was the one who went to America and opened the Cotton Club. (They made a film about it, with Bob Hoskins playing him, and his mate Frenchie was Fred Gwynne from *The Munsters*.) Madden got Carnera the boxer over from Italy; he got Mae West and put her in shows. The big musicals were on Broadway but the Cotton Club was in Harlem, with all the top bands there – black musicians who had to come in the back door, as that was the way it was run then. 'I rode shotgun with him when he used to take the booze down to different places [in the twenties],' said George. He was walking across the pavement when a rival gang opened up on them and shot two guys; he was right there in the thick of it.

The twins wound up with some American people who were wrong 'uns – they were slipped into them. When they opened the Colony Club, Meyer Lansky (the Mafia's Jewish financier) was behind it. George Raft was just the frontman, the meeter and greeter. It was run by Lansky's firm: Dino and Eddie Cellini, the two brothers who are mentioned by Hyman Roth (Mario Puzo's fictionalised version of Lansky) as Dino and Eddie Pennino in *The Godfather: Part II* (1974) – 'I'll have them running the casino' – when it's his birthday and he's cutting the cake. They were real people; they used to run Lansky's casinos. I would go over and meet Dino. We used to walk round the street and he'd give me the envelope, for the twins and me, and the Nashes. We were copping a bit of money. We'd get it one time, the Nashes would draw it another – so we knew what they were fucking getting!

The twins were the worst trouble because they kept going down the Colony Club, taking fucking ugly people with scars down their faces and ruining the gaff. So, to keep their licence going, they put an ex-Old Bill on the door. He was photographing everyone coming in and out, getting them to sign the register. I met Dino outside: 'We've got to stop them coming down, Fred, bringing all these fucking villains down here! We're here to keep 'em out!'

Sinatra had been down there and they wanted to meet him and all the Hollywood actors. They wanted to be up the front, they couldn't keep away. I was trying to keep a low profile and go legitimate with the betting shops, the casino and the clubs, kids in boarding schools; I was trying to be a straight-goer.

The Krays did help some people, but they were strong-arming most. They didn't do a lot of good as far as I knew. I don't know of anyone who really benefited from knowing them. They were always bleeding people, really – in the clubs and bars they took over.

The other sidelines I had with my old firm were big, heavy bits of work but nobody knew it was us who was doing it; we kept very shtum about it all. We never started splashing our money around. The twins were the only ones who got my photograph taken with different people. We were getting invited out to all these dinners – bowtie, dressed up. Of course the women loved it, but we didn't want to go. They were getting us involved in these sorts of things, which was our downfall, really: being associated with them all. We should have kept ourselves to ourselves, low-profile.

Ronnie Kray went over to New York in April 1968, the month before the twins got nicked, but it was the Yanks who took him there – the undercover-copper grasses. They were showing him where the St Valentine's Day Massacre took place – which made them look like cunts, as it was in Chicago!

We raised a load of money up the river for the British Olympic Boxing Team to go to Mexico in '68, because

otherwise we wouldn't have been represented in a lot of divisions – which was a liberty, really. Mickey Regan and I were going out there. That's John H. Stracey on the left, the Olympic champion, and Johnny Cheshire to my left, who was around me quite a lot down the pub and the 211 Club. Nicky Carter, on the end, wound up with his own company in the City. I had tickets to go to the Olympics but couldn't do it – I'd got fucking nicked with the twins! But Mickey went and while he was out there he got Montezuma's revenge. He wound up in the hospital with food poisoning and nearly died.

After the Colony Club, the twins fucked up everything that they touched: the casino in Knightsbridge; getting mixed up with politicians – they've put an additional thirty-year notice on some of the evidence surrounding that because it's too fucking hot. With the Lord Boothby business – and more on that later.

Ronnie didn't hide the fact that he was what he was. He came over to my pub: 'Ooh, I like these little bank robbers you got over 'ere!'

'Now, don't you fuckin' start all that!' I said.

I couldn't believe what he was saying; I thought it was a joke. But the twins used to argue like two fucking women:

'You bitch!', 'You slag!' You don't call a man a 'slag' – or at least you didn't in those days.

All the firm used to call them 'Gert and Daisy', or 'the Brothers Grim'. But they were vicious and evil, wicked bastards. They were in their own fucking world that they couldn't see out of, and they thought they were something special. There was nothing special about them, but they met Sinatra's son, Judy Garland, Sophie Tucker, Billy Daniels – all these American people. They were becoming famous and believing their own hype.

The Twins had these parties where everyone was constantly going off to the bedrooms. It was all too much for me. I couldn't get out of there quick enough!

They were all off in the bedrooms, having their nonsense. Dingdong Del and I seemed like the only straightgoers there. I said to him, 'This is *not* for me!'

Frankie Warren, the promoter's father, was there that night, too. He said to me in the toilet, 'What the fuckin' 'ell's goin' on 'ere?'

'You wouldn't believe it, would you?' I said.

Priests and politicians, it's a different world out there. They're just dealing with it now: I knew a girl who worked in the Home Secretary's office and she said one of them was a paedophile. This was back when I had the pub. I said, 'Don't tell me, I don't wanna know.' But it won't die; it keeps raising its ugly head.

The reason the Krays killed Jack 'The Hat' McVitie in 1967 was that they wanted him to go and kill Leslie Payne.

*Reggie Kray finally breaks his silence and reveals McVitie's watery grave*
# JACK THE HAT'S WITH THE EELS AND CRABS

JACK 'THE HAT': Butchered in basement flat

(Payne was the Krays' financial adviser, who introduced them to long-firm fraud. He became their enemy after removing himself from the Kray firm.) But he never did it, because the place where Payne lived was security-controlled. So, he's taken money for it and he's done the money on booze and drugs: 'You're off the fucking firm now. Fuck off, Jack!'

Sometime later they meet him; they've made a decision to take him back. But, before they told him he could come back, he's got a little team round him and he's running around saying, 'I'm gonna do the twins!' He even mentioned it to me at one stage.

'Don't talk like that, Jack,' I told him.

'I'm not fuckin' frightened of them. I'll fuckin' shoot 'em!'

Then he's at my club in Balham. I get called out and he's having it out with the croupier – but, before I get there, he throws his knife under a table, where a couple are sitting. It was a Scottish boxer and his wife, having a drink and something to eat from our free buffet.

I said, 'Come on, Jack, get out! I wanna speak to you.'

'What, and get a bullet in the 'ead, like Ginger Marks?'

'Never mind about that. I'm goin' downstairs to have a light ale. I'll give you ten minutes and, when I come back, I wanna see you gone. Get out of 'ere and don't come back again!'

He'd pulled his knife on the croupier because he'd done his money, he thought he'd been robbed. The people with him were a little crew from over Notting Hill. They were all round the table, gambling: 'Come on, Jack, you better go.'

'I ain't fuckin' goin' . . .'

'You'd better go 'cos it's serious, you'll get 'urt. We don't want no trouble 'ere . . .'

They talked him out of it, the bastard!

So this gets around and everyone is saying he misbehaved at the 211 Club. Ronnie Kray gets to hear of it and he's going off. So this is going on behind the scenes and then Jack goes to the Regency Jazz Club (a popular venue in Stoke Newington, where he lived), but I didn't find this out until *twenty* fucking years later!

Bertie Summers and another guy were on the door; Bertie later met me in my Gregory's pub, The Punchbowl, and wrote on a piece of paper exactly what happened that night. Jack came to the door; he was drunk and they wouldn't let him in. Under his coat he had a sawn-off; there was a bit of a scuffle on the door.

'Any of them Krays in there? I'm gonna fuckin' shoot 'em! Any of the firm in there?' he said.

He was going to shoot *someone*. They struggled with him. The gun went off and blew a fucking hole in the door!

Well, Reggie Kray was in there – he was sitting at the end

of the bar, rotten drunk. This was after his wife Frances had died and he was drinking himself into a stupor. If Jack had gone in there he'd have shot Reggie, that's for sure. But they forced him out and got the gun off him. They put the gun in the cloakroom.

Reggie came down and said, 'What was all that about?'

'Some drunk tryin' to gatecrash.'

They hushed it all up, didn't say it was Jack at all.

**FRANK:** Reggie (above, with Freddie, Charlie, Henry Cooper and Sulky Gower) wasn't 'the man'; he seemed to be more and more in thrall to Ronnie. He was taking a lot of purple hearts. That's why he got involved with McVitie, who was always taking them, and that's why McVitie was saying silly things. Not only that but he was drinking more.

He was going out drinking with Tommy Cowley at the nightclub where Nosher Powell used to be the doorman. I heard him shouting there one night. I don't know what was happening, but some people were ducking him by then.

**FREDDIE:** Reggie went away, satisfied, but word got around. So, they got him on the phone and said, 'Come back, Jack, we got some work for you to do.'

But he turned round in front of the two of them and said, 'You've only got me back on the firm because I come out to shoot you the other night!'

Reggie and Ronnie looked at each other as if to say, are you fucking sure? Now they know what happened on the door: Reggie would have been a goner.

So, of course now they're plotting to do him. They got Tony and Chrissie Lambrianou to bring him to a party, but what cunts they were! They had a roomful of people, young girls and young boys! I think they intended to batter him and really hurt him, but not to kill him. Still, they did say, 'Bring the gun.' But all the guns they had were from the Yanks, and they were fucking useless. That geezer was giving them all duds! (The mysterious American Alan Bruce Cooper was the Krays' armourer by this point.)

Knowing Ronnie, I reckon he might have gone through with it, but now they were going to batter McVitie. They had a screaming match with him first of all. Then Ronnie smashed a glass in his face.

Jack's taken his coat off to have a fight with them; he's got a silk-lined waistcoat on. One witness statement said Reggie was pushing a knife in and it was bending in the silk lining, so it wasn't going in. Then the other witnesses were saying he went out the room and they told him to fuck off, but he came back in to have a fight with them.

Jack was that type of fella, all pilled up. He could have walked out of the room that night, but instead he came back in to have a row. Because he could have a fight, Jack, he could walk on his hands around the room – he was strong, with powerful shoulders. In that Krays film (1990), he was a frail little weakling, but he was fitter and stronger than they were. He had no fat on him and he was on amphetamines all the time.

But there was no premeditation among the people who brought him, the Lambrianous and Ronnie Bender. Bender was silly because he got the knife from the kitchen for Reggie – that's why he got twenty years, whereas Tony and Chrissie got fifteen. Bender joined in the fight with Jack as well; even two little croupiers were having it in the fight until it got really serious. That's when they realised it had got out of hand. They reproduced their statements in Martin Fido's book, *The Krays: Unfinished Business*, which confirmed that the twins didn't really want to kill him that night.

They tore Ronnie Hart (the Krays' cousin) to pieces in the witness box because it wasn't him who came over to me: it was that little bastard who ran with them, Tommy Cowley. He was the one who came with Charlie.

Lant Street was right off the Borough and there on the corner was my pub. Hart said they parked on the corner and he saw Charlie go round to me; I opened the window up and looked out; I opened the door and let him in – for him to tell me they'd dropped Jack McVitie's body down in Bermondsey, the other side of the Borough.

They put it on my plate. They were supposed to go round Cazenove Road, near where Jack the Hat was murdered, and throw the body onto the railway track – that's what Ronnie Kray told them to do. But instead of that they drove him from Stoke Newington, through Dalston and Bethnal Green, right down through the Rotherhithe Tunnel via Commercial Road, out through the tunnel, and dropped him right round the corner from my pub!

How they did it at two or three in the morning and got away with it, I don't know. They just dumped him outside this church, where there had been a wedding the previous weekend.

The Krays went mad when they found out what they'd done. That's when they knocked up Charlie and got him out of bed to come over to tell me.

Hart couldn't possibly have seen this happen from where he said he was. He said I'd put my head out of a window, which was screwed down, where it was used as a broom cupboard. He knocked on the door of the pub, which never had a knocker on it (it had a bell at the top, which you had to stand on the step to reach). There were so many discrepancies. It was impossible, given the map of it all, for him to see round corners. Where he said he'd parked was too far back, so all his evidence was fucked.

But they accepted his evidence, and then Harry Hopwood came in afterwards and said that, after the murder, Reggie

Kray went back to his flat with a cut hand. They bandaged his hand up and then Hart fell asleep on the settee. He stayed there all night and didn't get up till the morning – and yet he's supposed to be coming over to my pub.

It was that little bastard Cowley – and they got the information out of him because he walked out of the case and got about six months. So he definitely rolled over and helped them, without a doubt. I never saw him again.

Bender made a statement as well, about bringing the body over and leaving it there. But they're all in the nick with me, making out that they're shtum and have said nothing. All three of them had made statements, and it didn't come out until all those years later when it came into the public domain. Fido got it from the Home Office. If they'd have produced that evidence, it wouldn't have been a premeditated murder: it would have been a row at a party that went wrong. But they never produced the prosecution statements, which was wrong. They should have given it to the defence counsel – that's how the Guildford Four would get out, because the prosecution never produced their statements.

And the fucking forensic evidence was laughable! The forensics officer said they dragged the canal, but got to a bridge and couldn't move because the council had put bollards there. But the firm went down there and threw the gun and the knife, wrapped in a tea towel, into the canal.

The divers go down there and come up with a gun with a hollow wooden barrel. It had a faulty mechanism. If that gun had been in there for the eighteen months since the crime was committed, it'd been in there *twenty years and eighteen months*! Someone must have thrown it away after the Second World War. It had disintegrated, whereas the gun would have been in one piece and the butt would still have been intact.

The things the prosecution got away with were unbelievable. The trial was a farce from start to finish. I was amazed at the evidence they were bringing against me from this bloody Hart. I knew he hadn't been there and it was completely false. Okay, the rest of it was true, but how did they fucking know this? It had to have come from Tommy Cowley, who ended up in Brixton Prison with Charlie. Reggie, Ron, myself and all the others were put into Wandsworth. Simply put, Cowley was a spy for the police.

As for Jack, he got a burial at sea.

Later, they even tried to put Lord Lucan down to me! John Pearson said he left his car at Newhaven and that was the last they saw of him. He left ten grand behind to pay off these criminals to get him out of the country, and he left across the Channel. But supposedly he was shot, and Pearson referred to this little 'facility' of Freddie Foreman's in *The Times*. There was a picture of me and everything, trying to put it on my plate!

I was in the nick when it happened, doing a ten for Jack the Hat.

**FRANK:** Freddie was a schtummer. Even Nipper Read, who nicked the Krays, didn't know who Freddie Foreman was – that was how deep he was. And if he had a big tickle, say, for fifty grand or a hundred grand of gold bars, he'd keep the same old car, wouldn't look flash, do his own thing.

He had his pubs and mansion houses, he'd stick money into them, but everyone who didn't know him just thought he was a good bussinessman. He never let on; he kept a low profile.

In his book, *Gangsters, Guns and Me*, Jamie Foreman blames Reggie and Ronnie for getting him nicked with The Hat. It was all a fit-up, but he got away with a lot of other things.

# PART TWO

## THE LEGEND OF THE KRAYS
## BY FRANK AND NOELLE KURYLO

I went in the Army on 7 May 1957. I used to come down to London from Leeds a lot because my Auntie Frances lived in Kensington – when I was a kid she wanted to adopt me. So, I used to wander round London when I was fifteen, sixteen, seventeen . . . I would buy my shoes and shirts in good shops; my parents were tailors, so I was always suited and booted, always smart.

I did my National Service from 1957–59. I first used to go into the Krays' Double R club in '57. I went in there with a couple of younger lads, who were stationed with me. That was the first time I saw Reg and Ron. When I went to the toilet and one of them was there, I couldn't work out how he beat me back so quickly; he just seemed to appear. That was the first time I set eyes on both of them.

And I kept going down to London – I used to go to my auntie's if we had a forty-eight-hour leave pass. I'd go down to the club where Christine Keeler and Mandy Rice-Davies worked.

When I came out of the Army, I went back to training a little bit, played a bit of rugby. But I got out of that as I was coming to London too much. I found a mentor called Joe Freeman – 'Cockney Joe' – who used to be a very good card sharp. He used to work card games in clubs all over Britain; he'd put a 'combination' in a shoe – in a baccarat shoe or a chemy shoe there are about eight packs, but he used to do combinations so he knew what was coming out and he'd always win.

That's what I used to do for years and years – Jack Spot was his minder before me, during the war. So, I'm staying down in London with Joe. He'd tell me, 'See me later, see me sparingly.' He never wanted me to get too pally with the Krays: 'Keep them at arm's length 'cos they'll turn on you.'

'I'm not bumming myself up, but I can take care of *them*!' I said.

I didn't see the strength of them, but I said if they were street fighters I could bang 'em both. But I used to listen to him and, when I'd see them, after ten minutes I'd have to step away from them. I always had a few quid on me, but they could never get into me. I'd never get involved because I could always make my own money. Even then, when they were in their twenties, I could see the way they were going; the only thing the Krays did was use. They used you and abused you, and that was all they ever did.

When the Krays started the firm, they all said that they demanded the first billiard hall and blagged that fellow. But I've got the contract at home where the Krays signed for the billiard hall on a proper deal. It was never blagged, they never fannied him, they paid him so much a week – but that was the only time they ever did.

In the other club they had, The Hideaway, they were like squatters. They were taken to court over Hew McCowan (the twins were remanded on a charge of demanding money with menaces in 1965). They had cards printed – 'Ronnie & Reg Kray' – but they never put any money in. I want to put this over so you can get the size of them: they were just thugs. People talk about the Regency Club, where they lured Jack the Hat from, but that wasn't theirs: it was run by two brothers called Barry. The Krays blagged them, they were frightened to death. The twins just used to move in and take over. The only club where they put anything in – it was a grand, God knows how – was Esmeralda's Barn. Freddie can tell you: *he* got them that club, not their financial adviser Leslie Payne.

I met a chap who was their godfather, name of Geoff Allan. He was a builder in Surrey, Essex, all over the place. His buildings were all grand but occasionally he'd set fire to one and burn it down. He was their mentor and any time there were any murders – McVitie or any of the others – they'd go to see Geoff at his mansion.

Geoff died in '98. I got most of the photos in this section of the book from him.

When Ronnie escaped from Long Grove mental hospital in Epsom in 1958, he stopped at Geoff Allan's. They had a photo of them in a big farm kitchen. In those days Ronnie had his hair cut short at the sides and so did Reggie, so that they could swap places (Ronnie's escape from mental hospital was effected by Reggie pretending to be him).

Geoff was the man who told them what to do. The morning they got nicked in '68, Mrs Kray phoned him up because she was staying at his big mansion in Hadleigh, Suffolk, in a cottage in the grounds. The twins were at her London flat – that was where they got nicked. She said, 'Can you get down here, Geoff? There's loads of stuff of Reggie and Ron's, all photos.' If the police had got hold of them, it'd be like having a birthday.

So he sent Terry Stace down, who was his right-hand man. They kept the photos and eventually Geoff bestowed all 300 to me. Most of them have never been seen.

Geoff Allan bought Gedding Hall, a big mansion in Suffolk. Bill Wyman, the Rolling Stones' bassist, lives there now. In his book, *A Rolling Stone Gathers No Moss*, he says that when he went to buy the house he looked on the mantelpiece and there was a photo of the Kray twins. Geoff said, 'I'm their godfather.'

He bought the house for £42,000 in 1969, and it's worth about £8 million now. But this is the strangest thing: when The Hat was killed in the basement where they were having a party, there were about twenty other people there, including Geoff Allan and his wife, Annie. They left the party about an hour before the murder.

But, when he found out what Reggie had done, Allan went berserk: 'You fucking clowns! What are you doing?'

There were two 'Kray firms', as the papers called them. The first was from 1960–65, and then there was a second, from 1965–68. But I must say many of the stories were smoke and mirrors; a lot of it didn't happen. They wanted to put out that they knew John Bindon, but they never did. I knew John well – coming out of borstal, getting nicked for this and that. He'd just got into films in '65 when they started murdering and Bindon didn't want to know them.

(Bindon was a thug, convicted killer and sometime lover of Princess Margaret. But he was also a character actor, taking supporting roles in the classic Brit-gangster movies *Performance* and *Get Carter*, and also appeared in *The Sweeney* TV series.)

The original Kray firm at the Double R club was the two Osbournes: George 'Ozzy' Osbourne and Colin 'Duke' Osbourne, who was known as Pasha. He was Freddie Foreman's pal but they almost got nicked together over a consignment of puff (Freddie later found out in the newspaper that he'd killed himself). Then there were John H. Squibby, Dicky Moughton, Billy Donovan (who was at the billiard hall when they went there to fight with some dockers – he was one of them and some were badly hurt), Fat Pat Connolly, Tommy Brown, Dickie Morgan and Mickey Fawcett. Fawcett wrote a book (*Krayzy Days*, 2014) that's really thin, but tells a lot of stories. He was close to them, as was Teddy Smith, but pulled away after the first murder when he realised he didn't want to know. They tried to kill him after that.

The second Kray firm was from 1965–68: Chrissie and Tony Lambrianou, Ian Barrie, 'Scotch Jack' Dickson, Cornelius Whitehead, Ronnie Bender, Albert Donoghue and Ronnie Hart (who used to work together) and the three Teale brothers: Bobby, David and Alfie.

Then there were 'floaters', who weren't on the firm but did their own thing: Harry 'Jew Boy' Cope, Bobby Clark, Billy Exley, Eric Mason (who was a pal of mine), the two brothers Teddy Berry (the boxer, who had his leg shot off) and 'Checker' Berry, whose proper name was Henry – he used to go checking the merchandise on boats on the Thames.

Bobby Teale wrote a good book (*Bringing Down the Krays*, 2013), but he said Frosty, Ronnie's driver, was killed – Frosty was still alive a fucking year ago! I've got the trial papers here and I can see what's happened: on the day after Ronnie killed George Cornell, the oldest Teale brother went secretly to the law and grassed 'em. He got hold of Chief Superintendent Tommy Butler, who did the Train Robbers. All they kept saying to him was, 'Don't mention homosexuals in your statement' because of what happened with Lord Boothby and Tom Driberg (respectively, Conservative and Labour MPs, both part of Ronnie Kray's gay underworld – Boothby notoriously so, as he was brazen enough to win a £40,000 libel payout from the *Sunday Mirror* for associating him with the Krays in 1964).

There was a big fear the Boothby story could bring the Government down. There was a news editor, Derek Jameson, who said, 'We've got the Krays, we've got 'em now!' And his editor said, 'Don't do anything, leave 'em alone' – and the police backed off for two years. But Tommy Butler was into it; he got a load of information and all of a sudden, after a year, it went missing. It rattled him; it shocked him. Nobody mentioned it in court in '69, but they should have asked Nipper Read, 'Why didn't you have a statement from the man who was dealing with the inquiry before you?'

I was minder for Danny La Rue (he was a popular English variety artiste and drag queen) for seven years, and I took the job off the gangster Billy Howard. But I used to nip off to see the twins and sorted one or two people out for them, 'straight' people. One was a really big titled man, who was having it off with a bloke called Clive Peterson, who Ronnie Kray was also having it with. He didn't get a slap, just a really nice warning.

Danny used to say, 'Frank, I don't mind you mixing with 'em, but *you do realise . . .*'

When Danny got his own club – from 1964–72 – they moved in to get protection money. It's in Nipper Read's book that an actor and his manager were about to open up to him, but, the next time he went, their solicitor was there and they wouldn't say anything. That was Danny, and that was when I pulled away from him because I didn't want to get in the middle of Reggie and Ronnie and him. I got pally with 'em all, but I stepped away from that.

Danny got chinned one night by Charlie Mitchell, who would turn Queen's evidence against the Krays (for the rest of his life Danny would have a big scar on his chin). Mitchell was the one who stood up in court and laughed at the twins. He was a very wealthy man, who went to Nipper Read when he nicked 'em – 'I've gotta tell you this, I've gotta get out of this: they've given me £5,000 so they can get a hitman to kill you.'

Mitchell later got killed in Spain.

I earned plenty of money with the twins, both when they were free and in prison. For the film *The Krays* they got a big lump, but they should have got more. They went through a couple of businessmen and me in Yorkshire; Lloyd Hume and I even had property with them in Puerto Banús.

I would go to see Mrs Kray with Cockney Joe. I used to go with him to stay at nice hotels, stop at the racecourse, and one day he said, 'Do you want to come and see Violet?' He used to help her out with money. He told Reggie to write to me but I couldn't go to see him when he was in Parkhurst. He couldn't have visitors unless they were relatives.

I started doing business with the twins again after their first book *Our Story* was published. It wasn't a success, and Noelle and I had to sell a van full to market traders and second-hand book shops. But then he did others: *Reg Kray's Book of Slang* (1989), *Born Fighter* (1991), *Thoughts of Reg Kray* (1991) and then, in 1993, *Villains We Have Known*, with me. When they were in the nick, I used to help them out left, right and centre – but you had to keep on top of 'em.

'[Frank Kurylo] was one of the best knuckle fighters from the fifties to the seventies, and his attire was immaculate. Frank came from Leeds, so in a way it was quite unique how the London crowd took to him . . . Frank was a good and loyal friend to Ron and I, and still is to the present day.' Reg Kray in *Villains We Have Known* (N.K. Publications, 1993)

These pictures of the twins as babies are all from the family collection. They were born on 24 October 1933, in Stean Street, Hoxton. In the previous year, their mother, Violet, had given birth to a beautiful little girl with thick black hair, who died very soon afterwards. They named her baby Violet, too.

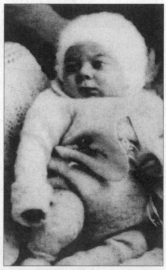

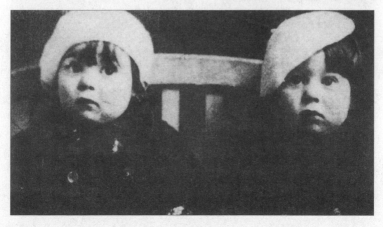

The story is told in a book by the twins' cousin, Rita Smith (*Inside the Kray Family*, 2008), but I first heard it from Laurie O'Leary, who'd written a book, *A Man Among Men* (2002), about his friend Ronnie. It's believed the baby died because Charlie Kray Senior was knocking his wife around. He used to batter her, which was why Reggie and Ronnie didn't like him. I couldn't understand why they didn't kill their dad – if somebody did that to my mother, I know what I'd have done to him.

The twins had healthy childhoods until they contracted diphtheria, from which Ronnie nearly died. One year later, the family moved to 178 Vallance Road, Bethnal Green.

This picture shows Ronnie and Reggie, aged eleven, on the boxing team at Daniel Street School in 1944. They're sitting either side of the trophy holder; Reggie has a straight back.

Above left Ron and Reg are fighting each other, three years before Reggie became Great Britain Schoolboy finalist. Above right records their first public bout in Stewart's Boxing Booth at Victoria Park in the East End, an all-comers prize-fighting contest.

One of Reg's favourite punches was the cigarette punch. He would offer the person a cigarette and as they leaned forward for a light he would throw a left hook. But, if he looked like he was going to try it with me, I'd have a vein in my head standing out at the side when I used to tense my jaw. I knew all about boxing, inside and out.

The Krays' pro boxing careers lasted less than six months. They turned professional on 3 July 1951 and their last fight was at the Albert Hall on 11 December 1951. About six months after that they went in the Army.

Reggie had seven fights; Ronnie had six and lost two. Later in the fifties our paths kept crossing – I couldn't understand why they never kept training. I think Reggie would have been British champion; I don't think he'd have

been a European champion. Charlie never trained and that's why he lost more fights than he won.

Ronnie was just wham-bam-thank-you-ma'am aggressive, didn't put any thought into anything. Reggie was a classy boxer – he could move, slip punches, turn you round on the ropes. He had a right good trick as well: as he bounced off the ropes he would use the momentum from the ropes and meet his opponent halfway with serious force. I used to see them at the fights at York Hall and various places.

Reg and Ron with their mum, Violet, in the backyard of Vallance Road in 1950. And overleaf is the twins shortly after turning pro (1951). That's Teddy Berry on the right, a good boxer himself, who later had his leg shot off.

Ronnie (right) aged twenty-one at the Regal Billiard Hall in 1954, with young friends. Laurie O'Leary grew up with him and he used to say to me that he could never understand the young boxing lads that he bedded, who were straight.

Reggie was fighting it. Geoff Allan said he used to take his boyfriends to whatever house he was staying at, whether Gedding Hall or in Walthamstow.

They were both homosexuals, but Reggie was trying to fight it all his life. Ronnie didn't give a shit. He once made a pass at me.

'I'm not like that, leave me alone or we'll end up falling out,' I told him.

'I was only kidding.'

'Yeah, like fuck you were kidding!'

When I was with Danny La Rue I used to see all sorts of things – Ronnie had an affair with Danny too.

When I was managing a cabaret club in Leeds I had a singer in called Clive Peterson. He was one of Ronnie's paramores and Ronnie was looking for him; he'd come up noth to get away from them. Clive asked me if I could straighten things up between them.

So I paled them up for a while and they had an affair for a bit. Ronnie was very jealous: if he met someone, he wanted to be with them 24/7, but he loved them to death. He was very domineering, strong, but he could never get to the next stage. In the 1973 book *The Brotherhood* by Leslie Payne, he says that, if they left Ronnie, he went to pieces.

He was an enigma: will the real Ronnie Kray please stand up, which is it? He was perplexing. If Ronnie made an arrangement to meet you in London in two years' time at the cathedral, he'd be there.

With Reggie, if he made a plan, forget it! Reggie would let you down. If Ronnie made an arrangement, if he wasn't in that state of paranoia he'd be there. Even the lads, all the villains, liked Ronnie better than Reggie.

Reg was sneaky. He always looked quizzical, always looked as if he was up to something. Ronnie was potty as heck. But Freddie Foreman said this: when Reggie hit someone on the jaw he'd always get the first punch in. Someone who could hit him back wouldn't dare because the whole gang would jump on him. They were only 5 foot 8, 5 foot 9; they weren't big fellas, but the two of them together were lethal.

It wouldn't be a fair fight – I've seen them do all sorts.

This is Ron (overleaf, second from left) and Reg (right) when they've gone AWOL from National Service, on Brighton seafront. Second from right is Dickie Morgan, who turned grass on them. He laughed like a hyena, a right funny man. I didn't see him after they went to the nick – he just disappeared. They met him in the Army and when they deserted they went to his house in the East End.

Pat Butler is left and Pat Aucott centre. Billy Webb took the photo – he did a good book (*Running with the Krays*, 1995), but there's a lot of shit in it! He wrote that Ronnie killed George Cornell because Cornell once battered him in a club in the East End. That never happened. Webb was a big bull of a man, with a huge scar on his face. They

battered him in a pub once, but he went on the run with them from the Army.

I did a book of twenty photos of the twins, a big leather-bound album, about 8 inches by 12. There's a good one of them with baby Patsy Kensit (Reggie's holding the baby) – they were friends with her dad, Jimmy.

This is the twins with their pal George Osbourne (overleaf, left), from the earliest days of the firm. Another friend stands between the two of them (Ronnie is cropped off to the right). They blagged a fella for money in Swiss Cottage – he got three years and Reggie got two for demanding money with menaces. That was when they had Esmeralda's

Barn. Ozzy used to own Le Monde club – he was to die after going swimming on Brighton Beach and choking on his own vomit.

Ronnie Kray (overleaf) on holiday in the South of France in the late 1950s. He looks very slim here. What he'd later do was drink about ten to twenty bottles of brown ale a night, and he shouldn't have. But I always thought that nobody seemed to eat well. When I used to go out when I was young, I liked to have a meal and a few beers, but all the lads seemed to do was drink, drink, drink! And if they ordered anything it was a double spaghetti bolognese – always a double, never a single one.

They put Ronnie on pills for his schizophrenia, which may have altered his appearance, too. There was a bent doctor

who used to live on the Isle of Dogs, and Ronnie used to go down there for his tablets.

This is little Gary Kray (bottom), Charlie's boy, outside Fort Vallance, aged nine or ten, with Tommy 'the Bear of Tottenham' Brown. Gary was a troublemaker – I never liked him. He was always pinching off Violet and his aunties,

blagging money off people.

As he got into his teens and twenties he thought he could say anything, thought he was untouchable because he was a Kray. I remember telling him, 'If you keep saying that you're going to get yourself and your uncles into a lot of trouble.' He got a bit nasty with a pal of mine: he tried

to borrow some money off him and said, 'I'm going to get my uncle to shoot you.'

'You're going to say that to the wrong people,' I told him.

But Mrs Kray thought the world of him.

Tommy Brown was of Gypsy stock. His wife was a fortune teller and they lived in a caravan. Before he died, he used to have a greyhound he took to Gedding Hall to see Geoff Allan.

This is Cousin Rita (right) – who later wrote a book (*Inside the Kray Family*, 2001) – with Mrs Kray and Reggie at the Double R club in the late fifties. Violet was a lovely lady, but all the books say she didn't know – *of course* she knew what was going on! But it was sad to see her sons

later go missing from her life. Rita, you couldn't get to know – she was a bit snobbish. She used to leave you alone so I didn't bother with her.

Reggie is with George Osbourne and Tommy Brown at the Double R in about 1960. By this time it was a very successful club.

Violet and Charlie Senior are handing over money to the British Empire Cancer Campaign in 1961. The charities were all a scam – it was all to be Mr Nice

Guy! It was bollocks: half of it never got there. If they handed two grand over, the Krays would have kept a grand. But they weren't greedy that way, if you were in with them. I had a Rolex watch given to me by Ronnie that I've got in my safety box now. If you showed respect for him, provided you didn't take a liberty, he was all right. But if he could walk all over you then he fucking well would! Both of them would.

The Double R club, around 1959–60. Tony Snyder (left, with his poodle) was always pulling a gun and threatening to shoot somebody. Reggie chinned him and knocked the fuck out of him in the billiard hall. Georgie Woods (standing next to Ronnie) has a glass in his hand and a broken nose. He was a right good robber and got put on Dartmoor for ten years. See Ronnie's hand on his shoulder: that's to say,

'I'm with him.' They weren't anybody then and Woodsy was a main face at the time.

This was at the opening of the boxing gym above the Double R, in 1961. Henry Cooper was European heavyweight champion, famous at the time, but he always claimed he didn't know the Krays – yet there he is standing right in the middle of them. He later denied opening the club. I've got another few photos with Henry in them. He'd have known what they were doing, but of course they didn't start killing till '66.

This is an official function at Esmeralda's Barn on the middle floor, in 1961–62. I went there a few times. It's the site of the Berkeley Hotel now. There's the Lord Mayor in the centre; Checker Berry on the far left; Ronald Stafford (next to him) was a county surveyor, a big pal of Freddie Foreman's, who used to get them bullion jobs because he knew the runs, but he got nicked in 1967 when a plane in Jersey with a load of bullion was put down to him.

The Krays used to do charity shows for people – boxing charities, spina bifida charities, they'd do anything to jump in. But they'd take half the fucking money anyway! Royal Navy Commander Diamond (to the right of Ronnie) helped them get the Barn.

A drinking club in the West End, 1963. Back row, from left: Pat Butler, George Osbourne, the twins, pop singer Terry Dean and Curly King, who had a little gang of his own. Front row: Ronald Stafford, Mad Teddy Smith (behind Charlie Kray's arm), actor Tom Yeardy, who finished up working with Vidal Sassoon, the hairdresser, and Limehouse Willy – who got slashed by Teddy Berry after a falling-out at a club.

I knocked Mad Teddy Smith out. I used to go out with a girl called Cathy Donoghue (her sister Annie married Tommy Steele). She used to have a flat in Great Newport Street, just off Trafalgar Square. By this time we'd split up and I didn't see her much. I got a call from the Black Angus steakhouse underneath Cathy. The manager says, 'She's upstairs, they're having trouble with a chap.'

She had her boyfriend with her and Teddy tried to pal

*him* up. She wanted him out of her flat. I said, 'It's not *the* Teddy Smith of the Krays, is it?' This was after their 1965 court case.

So, I went up and said, ''Ello, Teddy, it's time you were going.'

If he took his jacket off there was nowt about him, it was all fucking pads. So, when I chinned him, I wasn't chinning somcone who was a tearaway – my daughter's lad would beat him even now. It was a little flat and I thought he was going to come back in, so I hit him with a smart left hook.

The stairs were like a spiral staircase on a lighthouse. He went down three or four of them and I kicked him down a few more.

'I can't see, I can't see!' he said.

You had to press a button and a light would come on for twenty seconds. When he thought he couldn't see, the lights had gone off! By the time I put the light on he'd pissed off. And then he disappeared altogether.

The Krays put a lot of things about – they said they shot Teddy Berry's leg off. It wasn't them! They said they knew Peter Rachman (the notorious Notting Hill slum landlord) and he was 5 foot 10 – I knew Rachman well through my auntie, he was 5 foot 3 if he was stretching – and that they got five grand off him. It was bollocks!

When you put a load of shit into good stories, people believe it. Like when Selwyn Cooney was killed: Freddie Foreman said he got everybody on board to make sure they all 'saw' the same thing. It was also said that the Nash brothers went to the Krays – they had nowt to do with it.

Freddie said the Krays were too young, they were just up and coming, they didn't know anybody then.

Teddy Smith went to Australia after he disappeared in 1967, but everybody said he'd been killed and buried in Steeple Bay. I've got a friend Ray Rose, who went to see him and took photos. He said, 'Who do you think this is?'

'That's Teddy Smith, but he's old and bald!'

He had done some TV work, and even written a TV play in Australia. He'd done well for himself – he had a taxi firm and I think he wrote two children's books. It's just that, when he left, he never mentioned to anybody where he was going. He came home to London in 2000, before dying of cancer.

Reggie with his childhood friend, Laurie O'Leary, and Curly King (right) – a Teddy boy who wasn't much of a fighter,

just a toerag, really. But it was he who first called the Krays' home 'Fort Vallance'.

At the Society Club in Jermyn Street: if you look back at it as a snapshot of the sixties, you've got Jimmy Nash (second from left), you've got Christine Keeler and of course Ronnie Kray – it's almost like you've got the people there whom the Establishment would see as threatening the fabric of society. (They say Jimmy Nash is Freddie Foreman in some books and Freddie goes mad about that. That's Johnny Davies next to Nash.)

Next to Christine is Leslie Holt, who introduced Ronnie to Lord Boothby – because Boothby was having Holt. So, Ronnie said, 'Let's get 'old of 'im and 'ave some photos taken.'

Holt went to have a verruca taken off his foot but he died – the doctor gave him too much gas and he didn't come round.

The twins and Charlie (far right) with the actor Victor Spinetti and the Labour MP Tom Driberg (third and fifth from left) – two of Ronnie's homosexual clique. Then you've got the boxers Terry Spinks and Len Harvey (fourth and sixth from left). Dave Foreland (before Reggie on the right) was running long-firm frauds – he was a pal of Leslie Payne's. He shouldn't have been with him as he'd been a right straight fella.

(Payne asked me to do a long firm. He told me all about it and I had a meeting an hour later with Peter Rachman. Peter told me, 'You don't need it. You'll finish up wearing a paper hat.'

'What do you mean?'

'Like a clown. Leave it alone.')

The Clark brothers (black guys on the right) were dancers

– they used to have a studio at Tottenham Court Road. That's how the Krays got to know them, and they knew all the theatre people and a lot of boxers too. Reggie said in one of his books how not many people knew that they went for lessons at the Clark brothers' dance school. I think he made that one up, but he certainly shot their namesake Nobby Clark (second right) in the leg.

Mad Teddy Smith, Ronnie and Lord Boothby, at Boothby's house in Eton Square, Belgravia.

I looked after Danny La Rue for seven years and saw things I'd rather not mention. Everybody who was gay could get nicked then. There was an underground for homosexuals. People were 'cottaging' in the toilets.

Lord Boothby got a big whack of cash for 'The Picture We Cannot Print', 'The Story We Can Never Tell' in the *Sunday Mirror*. Who do you think finished up with the money? The Krays! Boothby was so much in debt that Geoff Allan said they got every fucking penny of it: 'If you don't pay, we'll shop you altogether' – and that would have been the end of him. Geoff got a whack of it; he said, 'I'll tell you, Frank, they had him by his bollocks!'

Just after that he married a young woman called Wanda Sanna to prove he wasn't homosexual. He also made a speech in Parliament, asking how long they were going to keep the Krays in prison on remand for the money-with-menaces charge.

This is Fred's loyal friend Bill Curbishley (manager of The Who) with Fred outside Roy Shaw's house on the morning of Roy's funeral. He went down for fifteen years for armed

robbery at one point; I think Roy was on the job with him. Reggie helped get him out after a good few years. They all said he was set up.

On the right is Freddie's godson Christian Simpson, and Steve Wraith from Newcastle is also pictured.

Ronnie is with the racehorse he bought for his mother, Solway Cross. On the left is the heavyweight Canadian boxer Larry Gains; on the right is Johnny Davies, who used to be a minder for Eddie Johnson, who owned the Two Puddings pub in Stratford.

Johnny and Micky Fawcett had to have it on their toes once to David Litvinoff's flat in Kensington. Litvinoff, a Jewish bohemian from the East End who associated with both the Swinging London set and the underworld, was

always in trouble with people but Reggie and Ronnie didn't slash him: he got slashed outside a tube station. Reggie said, 'We sent someone at him' – but they didn't. In some books it says they put a sword in his mouth – that never happened. Me and Johnny Bindon's pal used to see him a lot. In the film that Mick Jagger did with Bindon, *Performance* (1970), he was credited as technical consultant. Chas, the gangster character played by James Fox, is reputedly modelled on Freddie Foreman's enemy, Jimmy Evans.

Bobby Ramsey (left) got nicked with the Krays when they smashed up the Watney Street mob in 1956. Ronnie got three years and Ramsey got seven. After that he was Billy Hill's minder, then he worked for Billy Walker's brother George. He was a good fighter, but he used to write poetry and letters too. By this stage he was stuck into the unlicensed boxing circuit.

Eddie Pucci (overleaf, left) was a big American football star turned hitman for the Mafia. He was shot on a golf course in the States; they assassinated him.

Ex-world heavyweight champion Rocky Marciano (second from left) came over with Frank Sinatra Junior –

he was minding him when he appeared at the Talk of the Town. I don't know who the couple in between are, but the man on the right is the former gangster movie star and Colony Club host George Raft, a friend of the twins.

The first time I ever saw the Krays in '57/'58, they were wearing big overcoats that touched the ground – 'gangsters', both of them. They had great big padded suits. They were smart, but not city-smart, like bank managers and doctors are. Gangster-smart. When I befriended Ronnie he used to talk about Al Capone.

You never knew which one you were going to get: Ronnie could be teary-eyed and crying, a complete bastard or the strong and silent type (he just didn't know what to say unless he was doing business). He got on with Freddie Foreman when they were doing bad deeds.

Ronnie with Frank Sinatra Junior at the Rainbow Club, Finsbury Park, in 1963. Frank was pursuing a career like his sister Nancy, who was doing a bit of singing. He wasn't up to his dad or the other fellas, though.

Sammy 'The Yid' Lederman had an agency and Charlie Kray jumped in to take it over. He started getting stars coming across because he knew Barbara Windsor. Charlie just thought he'd have to go drinking with them – he didn't think it'd be a lot of hard work, signing cheques and reading contracts. Eddie Pucci and Rocky Marciano came through George Raft's Colony Club. They all just leapt up together. Geoff Allan had a big place he was doing up as a club for Raft and the Mafia to take over. He got nicked for setting it on fire a week after Raft was kicked out of the country.

Reggie Kray and his girlfriend, Frances Shea (centre right of table), at the Stork Club, Regent Street, London, in about 1963. Left of the table is William Frost – 'Frosty' – who was Ronnie's driver. He was supposed to have been killed in '67, but he was still alive in 2000. Connie Whitehead (third from left) used to run a long-firm fraud and the twins took it off him. He was in trouble, he got panicky, so he thought, 'I'm going to get nicked here.' But it was a bit of a torpedo for them. For some reason one of the firm was going to kill him, but the police stopped it.

This is Reggie at Vallance Road. He's got a great big gash on his lip – he'd had a fight with Ronnie the night before. Reggie said, 'You silly cunt, you'll get us all hung!' It must have been '64. They used to fight like fuck – 'You fucking slag!' they would call each other. But, once hanging got scrapped, they started killing people.

Frances Kray (née Shea) was very quiet. I couldn't understand why she wanted Reggie; even the vicar said their marriage (in April 1965) shouldn't take place. And Ronnie was always having a dig at her. Frances used to go up to Steeple Bay with the twins (as seen overleaf with Reggie). He could be a bit nasty to her, and tell her to leave his brother alone.

Just before they got nicked, Reggie had another girl, a blonde. But Reggie never made love to Frances. He liked women and he had plenty of birds, but Frances was a lovely girl and she shouldn't have been with him, ever.

Ronnie had tried to rape Frankie Shea, Frances's brother, just before she married Reggie. Frankie should have told his sister to leave them alone.

Over the years I used to visit Reggie in prison. He seemed to think the world of her. Then a woman wrote a book about Reggie and Frances (*Frances: The Tragic Bride*, 2014)

– the things he'd done to her! He put her in a hotel in Hyde Park and didn't go home for two days. What he wanted, I don't know.

She was a typist at an office, he used to go and meet her. But he wouldn't let her get a job after they got together. He did her in with his pushiness. She never used to take drugs but he got her into it.

Reggie had other girls straight after Frances killed herself. After Charlie got his ten years, he came out before everybody else; he had photos of Reggie and a woman called Christine Boyce. Christine wrote to him all the time – just before he died she was still writing to him in prison. I think she was the love of his life, not Frances, because Frances was treated like shit. He really did treat her badly.

Reggie and Frances Kray's wedding: 19 April 1965. Charlie and Dolly Kray and their son Gary are in the front row with the twins and the bride. Middle row: Mrs Shea (centre) and Violet. Back row: Frankie Shea Junior, Charlie Senior and Frankie Shea Senior.

I knew her old man – a very quiet man who worked for the Krays now and again. Mrs Shea was a bit of a loud-mouthed mother. Frances' brother was quite successful but, after the Krays got nicked, he finished up an alcoholic. He killed himself a few years ago.

World heavyweight champion Sonny Liston (centre) was allegedly killed by the Mafia via lethal injection; he died in 1970. Henry Simmonds (standing, left) was a big pal of Reg and Ron; he, Frank Warren and Jarvis Astair had the boxing tied up. His sister married Mickey Duff, the boxing promoter. Years later Johnny Davies (sitting, left) got a right tanning from the Tibbses, while he was in Spain waiting for his trial to come up. The Tibbs family were at one time considered the Krays' East End successors after the twins' 1969 conviction.

The twins on their way to court with John Squibb, on trial for demanding money with menaces from Hew McCowan at the Hideaway club in 1965. 'Squibby' came from a Gypsy

family; his father was a boxer. As a pal, he went back a long way with them. He went in and out of the firm.

Ronnie Kray with Mickey Morris (overleaf) at La Dolce Vita nightclub in Newcastle, 1966. That was when the murders started. I've got transcripts of the trial and one of the prosecutors said George Cornell was killed because he went to Mickey's brother and said, 'Do you know why he took him to Newcastle? He only went to bed the poor sod!'

After what happened at the Mr Smith & the Witchdoctor club in Catford, Cornell was the only one of the Richardson gang left at liberty. When it was all done and dusted, they knocked on Freddie Foreman's door: 'Let us in, there's been a bit of trouble!'

'What's happened?'

'Dickie Hart's been killed; Eddie Richardson's been shot; Frankie Fraser's dead' – they didn't know he wasn't. So, Freddie put them in flats all over London and one or two in caravans he had on the coast. Fraser always said Freddie set the whole thing up, but Freddie insisted he didn't.

As soon as the twins started killing, the original Kray firm made themselves scarce too. After the Cornell thing, Checker Berry and Billy Exley went missing. Exley had to have a gun at the side of him. The others went looking for him and asked, 'Why don't you join us anymore?'

'Fucking hell, they've started killing everybody!' he said. Straight lads, who were workers, had to physically prevent Ronnie from killing people every fucking night.

And that's why at the same time, in '66, they should never have lost Leslie Payne – because he was the man who got them all their money. He stepped away. Between Payne and Bobby Teale, they sent the Krays down with what they knew about them. Payne put himself in it: 'If you don't charge me, I'll tell you what I know.'

Little Geoff Allan was about 5 foot 2. He had a big mansion at Saffron Walden, Essex, with a load of antiques. You can see the twins there, and Bobby Teale says in his book, *Bringing Down the Krays*, that he went to the mansion after McVitie's murder.

Geoff was into frauds; he was into anything he could make a quid at. He was into doing up old houses, restoring them to their former glory, but then one would get burned down accidentally. Before he died, he said, 'I wouldn't mind a last go at what I used to do with Reggie and Ron. I'll tell you how it works: I'll buy a property, I'll put it in your name, say you buy it for twenty grand, we'll insure it for a hundred and twenty grand. Do a bit of work on it, and after three months it goes up and you get your money.'

So, we went looking and he said, 'This is a lovely one.' I've got a photo of the one we were going to set light to.

But I said, 'There's people living round 'ere, kids playing in gardens. If you set this alight, you'll catch all that.'

'Fuck it, we'll go somewhere else.'

We found a nice little one in Norwich and we had it all set up but he died just before we were going to do it.

Geoff was a villain, through and through. He liked to do insurance frauds above everything, but he had straight businesses: farms, shops, smashing restaurants.

I read in Jimmy Evans's book (*The Survivor*, 2002) that Ronnie shot a pig at Geoff Allan's farm. They supposedly didn't like the country, didn't know the country – they were in the country all the time! With Evans you've got to know how to pick out what's right and what's not. There's a lot of bollocks! Ronnie loved animals, so did Reggie. That's why we've got Ronnie with his dogs; when he was younger and he was pulled by the police he gave his occupation as 'dog breeder'.

That's former world heavyweight champion Joe Louis with his arm around Reggie,

at a personal appearance in a North East workingmen's club in 1967. Looking over Louis's shoulder is Alex Steene, a ticket tout from Leeds, who later passed his business onto his son, Greg. On the right, next to Ronnie, is Charlie Kray's pal, Tommy Cowley. He was a little sneak, a gambler – I never liked the fucking weasel!

On the left is Joey Pyle. He was a big guy, a fighter close to the Nashes. I got to know him eight years later. He was with the Nashes when they killed Selwyn Cooney at the Pen Club in 1960. Cooney was born in Leeds. There were two brothers, Selwyn and Laurie, and Laurie was my pal. I only told Joey I knew Selwyn later, before he died.

I was with Selwyn the night before he was killed. He had a gun with him and said, 'This is my equaliser.' He'd had a fallout with the Nashes over a prostitute girlfriend who'd bumped Nash's car. It was only seven and a half quid's damage, and that's what he got killed over – he'd given her a slap or something. That afternoon I rang Margaret, who he lived with, and she said, 'He's been crying all morning. The Nashes are after him.' So, why he went to the fucking club . . . But he could fight, he was a street fighter.

He was in the Pen Club with Billy Ambrose, Freddie Foreman's best pal – who was in Dartmoor and kept coming home on weekend leave when he'd opened the club. Selwyn was shot with his own gun. When it was all over, Freddie went to the Nashes and got everybody on the same page about what had happened.

Ronnie with friends in Barcelona in the early sixties. Pat Butler (white shirt) was the kid who screwed the takings from the collection box at the church where the Krays all got married and buried. I think Bobby Buckley (right) was

in military prison with them, but *The Sun* later ran this photo and wrongly said he was the *Bill* actor Billy Murray.

At that time Ronnie could get nicked over here for being homosexual so he'd have more freedom in a place like Tangiers, where he was photographed being driven by Ian Barrie in Billy Hill's MG, in 1966. Christine Boyce took that photo. I've got another one where they swapped over and she's in the driver's seat.

I met Billy Hill twice, with Cockney Joe. I just shook hands with him and he said to me, 'I'm sorry about what happened to your pal, Selwyn Cooney.' Hill said Selwyn would have been next in line – never mind the Krays, he'd have taken the lot of them. I had more to do with Jack Spot than Hill because he used to look after Cockney Joe,

though I don't know how the fuck Spot got to be considered a tearaway.

There was nowt about Billy Hill – he was a user of other people, but he'd slash them as well. He was really successful after doing about twenty-five years in the nick in dribs and drabs. He was a somebody, but to me he looked like a nobody. In terms of villains, the top man is Freddie. Hill was a smart man with a lot of good minders – he had Bobby Ramsey, George Walker, so it wasn't a matter of *him*, it was the people he had.

Ronnie and Dickie Morgan with Tony Bennett. The twins had just been locked up in the nick but were released in the mid-sixties. They weren't really villains as such. It's a contradiction, but they liked to be seen doing glamorous

things with stars. If someone had brought Rin Tin Tin along, they'd have wanted their photo taken with him – they just wanted to be seen.

As Freddie says, they didn't really like being villains, though they were in the nick all the time. They were disdainful of the middle class, of clerical workers or people from a family of substance, but the hierarchy of stars they had respect for. If you were a film star or a singer, they'd like to be with you. But I know Eric Clapton came to play at Esmeralda's Barn one afternoon, when he was with the Yardbirds, and Ronnie said, 'Fuck off, all of you! We can't hear ourselves speak upstairs!'

Eric Mason (author of *Inside the Underworld*, 2007) got the twins into La Dolce Vita in Newcastle. The three with

their backs to us were a Newcastle firm. This was the year before Dennis Stafford got done for the 'one-armed bandit murder', the killing of Angus Sibbet (the 1967 inspiration for Ted Lewis's 1969 novel, *Jack's Return Home* – which in turn provided the basis of the classic 1971 British crime film, *Get Carter*).

I knew Angus, did a lot of business with him. The Krays were on a retainer with the bloke who used to supply the clubs with one-armed bandits in London and Newcastle. He found out Sibbet was pinching money from him and he got shot. I know the Krays were there a couple of days before it happened – they didn't do it, but I got the feeling they were involved in it. All his life Reggie Kray slagged Stafford off – 'That cunt!' – and Stafford never liked Reg and Ron.

But he got fitted up. They couldn't even prove he was in the place at the time. He and his brother came back from Majorca that week, and that's when Sibbet got killed. I've got photos of the other guy who was done for the killing, Michael Luvaglio, at the gym where Reggie's standing next to him in '61.

Ronnie at the Talk of the Town (now the Hippodrome), for the birthday of former welterweight Ted 'Kid' Lewis (overleaf, right). He's with his old pal Sophie Tucker, an American singer, who was kind of a Mae West figure. Lewis was world champion when she was at the top of her form. To the far left of them is Duke Osbourne. I knew him – my pal used to buy drugs from him. Just like Fred, he could tell

a good story. He came from a good family but he was a bum chum of Ronnie; they were fucking each other.

Winston's club, 1968 (overleaf): just before the Krays' final arrest. Left to right: singer Leapy Lee ('Little Arrows'); actor/singer Tony Mercer (*The Black and White Minstrel Show*); Christine Boyce – who was in Reggie's bed when they woke him up and arrested him that morning; Reggie; Joe Wilkins, the club owner; Jimmy Evans, Wilkins's best pal; unknown; Tommy Cowley.

Evans was so lucky. Billy Howard was angry with him for what he'd done to George Foreman: 'Give that fucker a hiding!' He slipped out of Winston's just before we got there. He was a smallish fella but he was a dangerous little fucker. He had the needle, I think, because he was in a Mickey

Mouse firm and he thought the Foremans were involved in the Train Robbery: 'He was giving my wife ten-shilling notes to change.' Evans wasn't in the same class as Freddie in terms of being a top villain.

Ronnie in New York with Dickie Morgan (overleaf, left) and boxer Willie Pep, who was involved with the Mafia; they had him under their wing. The fellow on the end with the moustache grassed them up: Alan Bruce Cooper was an informer for the American police, trained up to get them nicked.

Everybody was shopping each other at the end. If you look at the Krays' case, everyone but the dog gave evidence against them. The Lambrianous did after they got weighed off: 'We shouldn't have said what we said, Ronnie *did it* and Reggie *did it*.' They turned after the case. Ronnie Hart

shopped them, Donoghue shopped them, the Teale brothers shopped them, Exley shopped them . . . They all bloody shopped them!

Ronnie in New York with Mafia man Joe Kaufman (he got nicked with them). Reggie broke Kaufman's jaw in the nick because he turned on them. He was reading a paper when Reggie did it.

Charlie Kray (right) got a ten for supposedly disposing of the body of Jack the Hat. It was '69 when he got weighed off, and he did seven. This photo came at Tony Lambrianou's (left) release in 1984, after he did his full fifteen. I met him once or twice, but I could never understand Freddie doing a book with him; he was a nobody. He did a job and went down for it – robbing a Wimpy Bar. But he was so unlucky to get fifteen years. He wasn't on the firm that long, and, instead of turning Queen's evidence like Donoghue, he kept quiet. Okay, he and his brother took Jack the Hat to get murdered, but he was just an also-ran. Had he turned QE and shopped them, he'd have got out of it.

But he got a living as soon as he got out the nick. Reggie phoned me and said, 'I've just seen an article on that cunt. He gave evidence against me at the end! After he got weighed off, he fucking went in with his brother and came out with the truth.'

Freddie didn't find out till after they'd done their book (*Getting It Straight: Villains Talking*, as told to Carol Clerk, 2002). Lambrianou started crying when they were working on it in his flat: 'I didn't mean to do it . . .'

'What made you do a book with Lambrianou? He wasn't in your league,' I said.

Freddie said he just wanted a partner to bounce questions off – a double act of comedians, one serious, one funny. 'What do you think, Fred?' he would say. Freddie would tell the story and Lambrianou would say, 'Yeah, that was it.'

Reggie Kray training in Parkhurst prison, Isle of Wight, 1991. I started visiting Reggie on the mainland because he could have visits only from his family when he first got weighed off. I went everywhere you can imagine – Leicester, Nottingham, Birmingham, about ten different prisons. I've got letters from him at every prison.

In Nottingham prison, I'd gone to visit him with Charlie and another fella called Brown – he was about 6 foot 2, he looked like Tommy Brown, a big lad. He was on the visit to try to get Reggie to sign an agreement for him to run a security business, at nightclubs, in their name. I got involved when he was guarding factories and warehouses.

Reggie wanted a private visit in the chapel. At the back was a big colour painting of Christ. He had his shirt wide open and we could see his six-pack. He was brown because he used to sunbathe. He never swore on prison visits, but he did this day: 'What 'ave you been fuckin' doin'?'

He was getting ready to have a go and pushed the corner of the table at me.

'What's your problem, Reg?'

It turned out that I'd taken a fella in with me who'd done a book and ripped them off. He thought I was covering for him, which I wasn't.

'I'll fuckin' knacker ya!'

'It won't do you any good in 'ere,' I said, because I had that big fella with me. 'If you let go at me, forget it.'

So I got up and walked away.

'Don't go, don't go!'

He followed me out and said he was sorry, so I went back and sat with him.

One other time he did that and I turned on him – told him to fuck off or I'd rip his head off. He said to my wife, Noelle, 'That husband of yours, he's a nutter!'

I have got a quick temper, but there was one thing going through my mind: you have to stamp on 'em before they stamp on you. He was fucking screaming at me – but maybe it was all bravado.

I thought he was going to put one on me before I sat down, but he didn't – he sat down too.

I visited Ronnie in Broadmoor dozens of times. Broadmoor isn't a prison, it's a hospital and they can get dressed up in their normal clothes – they have big, strong guards, that's all. Anything you had for him, you could leave at the desk: 'I've got a thousand cigarettes for him.'

'Just sign there and pass them over.'

(Ronnie Kray's death from heart failure, on 17 March 1995, has been attributed to his habit of chain-smoking between sixty and a hundred roll-ups per day.)

So, it was just a hospital they couldn't get out of. He had his suits on.

'What you want, Frank?' he used to say to me.

I'd have a coffee or a non-alcoholic beer. This fella in a white jacket would be working for Ronnie.

'Put it on my bill.'

Obviously he had his moments, but you saw him all dressed up in the best Savile Row suits, ties and shirts. I bought him three or four sets of ties and shirts but I made sure I was paid the money early. He'd always have a different suit and watch on – and his watches were nothing cheap. I had one given to me when he went to the nick, but he gave a lot away when he was in there. People thought he was doing it for favours, but he wasn't

He was a giver; he was a contradiction.

Ronnie used to say to Reg, 'Fuck prison, get in 'ere with me, it's in a different class!' But Reggie wanted to get out. Deep down, he thought he would. He said, 'If I get in there, Frank, I'll never get out.' But he'd have had an easier time.

Ronnie once said to me, 'I couldn't 'ack it in nick any more, I 'ad to come 'ere,' because he was getting into fights. He'd have either got killed or he'd have killed somebody. He lasted only about five or six years in regular prison.

When he was in Broadmoor, Ronnie wanted some ties made with 'Krays' on. So, I contacted a tie maker and shirt maker called Frank Rostron for him: he wanted a few samples done.

'We'll get 'em done in different colours, iron the exes out and send 'em in to Ronnie,' I said.

He got on the phone and bollocked me.

'These are samples, we've got to see if you like 'em,' I explained.

'I don't fuckin' like 'em!'

He put the phone down.

Next thing he's sending flowers to my wife, apologising: 'Sorry for what I said.'

But they needed me; I didn't need them. I used to get a lot of grief from Ronnie but it was the illness that did it. And Reggie had a bit of an illness – after thirty years it can't do your bloody brain any good.

**FREDDIE:** In Broadmoor, Ronnie did a painting of a cottage with a picket fence and a pathway – and a black sun. It was psychological. He dreamed of a white cottage home with a picket fence, but there's no sunshine.

**FRANK:** When Ronnie fell out with anyone, everybody was a slag: 'You *slaaag*!' I once went on a meet with Ronnie at Broadmoor and he said, 'What's that *fucking slag* doing?' This fella Pete Gillette had been sleeping with Reggie in prison, got out, and ended up with Ronnie's wife, Kate Kray.

But, really, I used to feel sorry for them when I drove away. I don't know how they did their time.

Ronnie wanted Lambrianou killed before he died. There

were stories going round that either he'd slagged Kate Kray off or they'd found out he'd made a statement later on. Ronnie was going on about this, but then he died.

A lot of people got in to Ronnie's funeral that shouldn't have, I don't know how. But it was a well-attended funeral. It was a lot better than Reggie's – that wasn't as big. Around the coffin at St Matthew's Church, Bethnal Green, are Charlie, Reggie, Johnny Nash, Freddie in the corner (second from right) and Ginger Dennis with his back to us. (Dennis was the one who slashed Jack Spot.)

On Bethnal Green Road it was just as if royalty had died; you couldn't move. We went just out of London to Chingford cemetery, but it took us an hour to get there. Everything was stop-stop-stop. I had a good talk with Steven Berkoff, the actor who played George Cornell, who got shot in the pub. Freddie was there, with his son Jamie.

I'm standing on the left of Reggie, who you can see in profile talking to my wife, Noelle (left). Les Berman was on the Kray firm – I think he worked as a market trader. That's him with his back to us in the green mac. Facing him to the right is Lambrianou. The guy with the beard on the right is a prison warder. Flanagan, with her back to us in the blue dress, was a hairdresser to Mrs Kray and also the first Page 3 girl.

I couldn't have done his time; I'd have ended it. All the shit you're in with, you can't pick the people you're stuck with for years. On the outside you wouldn't give them the time of day, never mind talk to them! How he got through it, I don't know.

Reggie had a few affairs in there. He had a gash on his eye

from when a young bloke he was sharing a cell with threw a pot at him during a lover's tiff.

I used to get him some spliff. I had to spend about fifty quid on a big lump that was shaped like a cigar in plastic, so it could go up his arse. I used to take it to the nick but I would not take it in – I'd pass it to someone and, if they got caught, it was up to them.

On the mainland I saw him in every prison you could go to, right to the end. He used to ring me up because I had cancer at the time. I'd started chemotherapy in '97 and I was just getting over mine.

The authorities knew he had cancer but they weren't treating him, they were giving him Gaviscon. That was all they were giving him in the nick. It was a terrible death that he had. In that TV programme that they did, *The Krays: The Final Word*, he was drinking whisky and morphine. I lived every second of it because I was like that when I had it bad.

I lost all my hair. I had mine for four years but now I was putting weight on – he used to ring me up and I'd say, 'Reggie, I can't tell you because it's a different type of cancer.' Mine was lymphoma and his was different altogether. (Reggie was suffering from cancer of the bladder and bowel, which eventually spread to much of his body.) So, I wrote a letter to the governor and we got a lot of people to write to the British Government.

The next thing is he's in hospital and they've set him free. The Government were trying to look nice, but they killed him off. He might have lived another year if they'd looked after him, but it was horrible what they did: he was in a cell without home comforts. I had my wife looking after me; I used to have my pet dogs around me. He was in a cell on his own – with nobody to cuddle, to kiss, to cry to . . . because you cry a lot.

I'm not excusing what he did in his life but he had a rough time, the poor sod. I've got a record, Tom Jones's 'The Green, Green Grass of Home' – I put it on sometimes and I cry when it says, 'I was only dreaming'; he was still in prison.

I always think of Reggie.

I went to the hospital on the day Reggie was dying, at Norwich. Bradley Allardyce (Reggie's gay prison lover in his later years, younger than him by decades) kept coming in and out. Serving nine years for armed robbery at the time, Allardyce has now been sentenced to life for murder.

'Can you tell 'im to fuck off when I'm talkin'?' I said.

He kept coming in to where Reggie was in bed, from a hallway in another part of the hospital. He's got newspaper people he's giving a story to, and photographs of Reggie. I told Reggie this just before he died.

'What are you fuckin' makin' excuses for this cunt for?'

He knew all the wrong people and they all abused him. At

the end of the day Reg followed his true nature by being bi-sexual. Geoff Allan said to me, 'His fuckin' melon's gone!' (he called his head a 'melon'). He wasn't like the man I used to know, but that's what the nick must have done to him.

Freddie went there to speak to him and hold his hand on the day, 1 October 2000, with Joey Pyle and one of the Nashes.

**FREDDIE:** Reggie Kray died in my arms. The wife (crime fiction novelist Roberta Kray, née Jones) fucked off out of the room, as did Allardyce, that poofy bastard Reggie was having it with. Him and her had been sitting on the edge of the bed. We'd been in there a couple of minutes, talking to Reggie – me, Johnny Nash, Joey Pyle and Wilf Pine.

We'd bought tickets to go to Norwich and she kept blocking us. Each time she knocked us back. Wilf said, 'We've gotta get down there, he ain't gonna last much longer.' So we sort of gatecrashed – she didn't want us there at all.

'Wipe his lips – his lips are dry and he's trying to talk,' Johnny said.

'I know how to look after him!'

She went right on the turn. The next thing you know, she and this Bradley have got up and walked out the room.

So, I went and took her place, where she'd been sitting on the side of the bed. He was trying to make a conversation.

'You 'ad a place up the road from 'ere – you're back on the old turf,' I said.

Which it was, they had a house in East Anglia.

He was saying, ''Ow did ya get down? 'Ow's Jamie?'

Then all of a sudden the doctor came in: 'I need to see the patient, I've got to give him an injection.'

'Don't go, don't go!' Reggie pleaded.

'We'll go in the bar an' 'ave a drink,' I said.

'I'll see ya later. Don't go, though!'

The doctor gave him his jab. When we go back up again, he's unconscious – he's gone. One minute he was talking rationally, the next he was *non compos mentis*, right out of the game.

So, I sat there and he was still trying to talk. I suppose he must have had his five jabs and the sixth one does you – that's what they reckon with morphine. You could see he wasn't going to come out of it. It was a terrible thing – he'd gone down to a skeleton by now.

He came round again; he looked at me and he tried to talk.

'Don't fight it, Reg, let it go! I'll see you another time and another place, mate,' I said.

I was trying to comfort him, holding him round the shoulders at one stage. He was silent for a little while. Wilf, Johnny and Joe were all standing by the bed.

All of a sudden he went, 'Uhh!' – and they all fucking jumped!

'I thought you'd gone,' I said.

But that was his last breath, the finale: he was finished.

Of course she came back in, and the doctors. We went downstairs and when we came out, all the press were waiting outside. I made a couple of comments and came back home.

She hated it. But how could a woman fall in love with Reggie Kray? He was homosexual anyway, and he was the most unlovable person you could ever fucking meet!

I'd spent time with him in Maidstone, when Ronnie died, consoling him – the screws came and got me because he was in another wing from me.

'Would you go over and keep him company because of the bad news he's had?'

'Certainly.'

So, I went over and stayed with him all day – it was St Patrick's Day, all the hooch that the cons had made was coming in, coloured green.

He had a little cry, talking about Ronnie, but you couldn't get close to him.

And then all the wife was doing was making trouble for everybody over the funeral. I couldn't go to it – I was in Horseferry Road, being interviewed by the fucking murder squad over Ginger Marks, more than thirty-five years after it all happened. And they wanted to know who was shot on the Battle of Bow – because Dighton, the guard who fired the shots, was worried he'd killed someone.

'No, tell him not to worry,' I said.

**FRANK:** There were a lot of people at Reggie's funeral but those who should have been in the church weren't there. The wife didn't want them there; she didn't want them carrying the coffin. Roberta organised it all, even down to the pall-bearers, and she didn't want any of the old firm there. It definitely wouldn't have been what Reggie wanted.

Whereas Dave Courtney – who's a smashing lad, plenty of chutzpah and bottle, good sense of humour – was the head man when Ronnie died, she got another one and it was a bit of a mess.

Half of the people didn't even turn up. She wanted Reggie to die as a nice reformed gangster but he wasn't like that – just a few months before he died, he wanted somebody killed.

It was a fella called Gillette who Reggie was having an affair with. Reggie's slagging Gillette off and he says, 'Come down and visit me – I want 'im done.'

But I said, 'I'll have to pay for what's got to be done – have you got any money left?'

'I've got fifteen grand left.'

I had it all set up – I was going to get Gillette a tanning. I wasn't going to kill him, but the money didn't come forward and Reggie half-backed off.

It was going to take me a week to get him into the right place where we'd do what we were going to do. But it died a death – and that was just before *he* died! So don't try to make out, 'He's got God in his life.' He *did* have God in his life. He had to lean on somebody so he leant on God, but he still had all that devilment in him.

# PART THREE

## THE LAST GANGSTER
## BY FREDDIE FOREMAN

We were at Table 4 in Wormwood Scrubs when I was doing my ten-stretch on the McVitie charge. There was a television right there in front of us, and one at the other end of the wing behind us. There were three hundred prisoners in there.

We ran the fucking wing; we kept it nice and sensible, we had our screws straightened and bringing in booze for us. We had a little scam with Gordon Goody going over to have his back massaged by this woman – she was a therapist. He had this poacher's jacket made with all these pockets. When he'd come back, they'd search him but in the pockets were all these steaks and pork chops with the kidney in them.

While he's having his massage behind a screen, all these other people are waiting their turn, the screws sitting there with them. We were all Cat-A'd up; I was double Cat-A. We worked in the laundry together – the best job in the fucking nick: you haven't got to go out in all weathers.

Jimmy Hussey was the chairman of the film club and we'd select the films we wanted to see every week. So we lived all right; we survived it all.

We used to get a bit of mescaline in and trip out on a Friday night, because it was the only nick in the country that banged you up at half past five of a Friday and didn't open up till the following morning. The governor said this was the time you could write your letters home to your families; that was what the idea was, so the screws could get away and have an early night. It was a very good scam, really! But, when I was in Leicester, the special units went on hunger strike because of the conditions we were living under: sleep deprivation. Every fifteen minutes they were checking you out in your cell, banging on the door if you didn't show your hands and your face. They were switching your light on and off, too. Then they went to the next cell and unlocked the bolts on the door. You couldn't have any sleep at all!

Then, on your visits, you'd have your visitors and your kids at one end, you at the other, and a screw with a notepad taking down everything you fucking said. The visits were terrible. We had to change into sterile clothing before we had one; they put metal detectors all over the visitors. If you put someone on your visitors' list they went to their employers and checked them out. The security was fucking ridiculous!

They called Leicester prison 'the Submarine' because it was so claustrophobic. They put a false ceiling in the cells;

daylight couldn't come through the windows because there were so many fucking bars, as there had been an escape attempt. The exercise yard was just a cage as you went through a tunnel; one door opened and the other one didn't – just like on the Security Express robbery. The conditions were so bad we all went on hunger strike; I ate nothing for twelve days, just had water. I could see my fucking ribs – I hadn't seen them since I was about sixteen! I was so pleased when it was over. They changed our conditions; we tidied up the Cat-A system a lot, made it more liberal.

I'd just got out of my ten. Jimmy Hussey and I (that's him sitting on the right, with fellow Train Robber Gordon Goody on the left – they hadn't been home long, either)

were opening up the Charlie Chaplin Club in Wardour Street, Soho.

It was all a bit hush-hush when we were taking it over; we'd been building up a nice clientele and having late drinking. We had a restaurant there, with some nice grub and a couple of girls. Maureen was behind the counter, with Jimmy's wife, Jilly. Maureen had the experience of serving in my pub.

It's going along lovely, but I'm going in there early one morning and I look at the placards on the pavement: 'TRAIN ROBBER OPENS SOHO NIGHTCLUB'. Jimmy Hussey's done an interview with the press.

Now, West End Central made themselves busy: if you were a minute over time you were fucking nicked, you'd lose your licence. They really put the pressure on us.

It was ridiculous because I was taking all the customers from the A&R Club late at night when they finished, when Mickey Regan and Ronnie Knight were running it in Charing Cross Road. I used to look after it when they had holidays; I'd run the club for them. They used to shut bang on time, but we would be there all night.

But the Charlie Chaplin Club was tucked away in an alleyway, a little court off Wardour Street. Upstairs was a walk-in bar and the club was downstairs. It was doing well, but the next thing you know we had all the headaches with the Old Bill and it just went downhill. Folded.

This is at a party at my house in Dulwich, in the early eighties. That's Freddie Puttnam, my brother-in-law, on

the left. Next to him is Stevie Ellison; he was a good little fighter whose parents lived next door to me. Those are the Hennessy brothers, Richard and Peter, on the right. But Peter got murdered: Paddy Onions stabbed him in the back at a boxing do. In return, Onions got shot outside his wine bar afterwards. Mickey Hennessy, the third brother, was shot in the neck because he was the danger man. Once his brother was killed, they tried to kill him as well, but he survived it.

Here, I'm going to Ronnie Knight's wedding in Marbella, Spain, in June 1987. In the documentary *Britain's Greatest Robberies* on the Crime & Investigation channel it's got this footage of my Jamie and me walking to the wedding. It has the Bank of America robbery and the Brinks-MAT; the Security Express (which I was involved with) was on first –

but I'm in it all the fucking way through! They've got family footage of when Gregory and Jamie were little kids, running around when I took them on holiday. I don't know where they got it – someone must have sold it on to them.

Here's Charlie Wilson (right), the Great Train Robber who was shot dead in 1990. I was in Brixton prison at the time. A lowlife who goes under the name Joe Flynn was interviewed and said I'd put a contract on Charlie over a drug deal. They tried to involve me again, but what Charlie was up to was nothing to do with me at all. Roy Adkins in Amsterdam was the one who put the contract on him, over Adkins's name coming up. He was on his toes in Amsterdam and got Danny

Roff from south London, who Charlie knew, to go and do it. Charlie's wife Pat let him in: 'Oh, he's out on the porch.' He just fucking walked round and shot Charlie, the bastard!

Of course, Roff got shot afterwards and crippled up. Later, when he was getting out of his wheelchair into his Mercedes, they shot him and finished the job. He didn't survive much longer; nor did Adkins.

My Georgie (centre) was shot with a shotgun in 1964 and Jimmy Allen (left) was murdered. He had his brain smashed in with a crowbar when he was asleep, in 1986. Jimmy had scrap-metal yards – we used to get acetylene bottles off him for cutting open safes and he'd dispose of motors if we wanted one cut up. He was a lovely guy; he used to love looking at engines and motors down at Puerto Banús on the boats. He'd talk to the captains: 'You're burning too much oil there,' he'd say, looking at the exhaust coming out of the ship. He was really knowledgeable. His yards sold for 600 grand; the council were buying them all up.

He earned a fortune.

The wicked bastard who killed him has never paid the price, although his son, Billy, was found guilty of defrauding £2 million from his father's company (but not of hiring a hitman with intent to murder his father).

This is my first apartment in Alcazaba; I ended up owning four, including a luxurious penthouse split over two levels where I lived. Alcazaba was a top-class complex and I had amazing views out over the port to the sea.

I was one of the first to go to the 'Costa Del Crime' – in 1982, after I'd returned from the States and got a two-year

suspended sentence in the Dukie Osbourne/Eddie Watkins case (see Part One). There's my George on the right, when he was working with me, then Ronnie Everett, Johnny Mason and me. We were three of the 'Costa Del Sol Five' – the others being Ronnie Knight, who'd been nicked at this point, and Clifford Saxe.

They brought it all on top, the Knight family; they were being kept under observation in their pub, The Fox, before the Security Express robbery (at Shoreditch in the East End in 1983), and the fucking garage owner they went round to – John Horsley, who rolled over straightaway – had nowhere to put the money so he put it in his father-in-law's council flat, in a 'secret cupboard'.

My name never came into it at all until I was in the El Alcazaba complex in Puerto Banus, Marbella, buying a flat there. Once I settle in, Ronnie Knight comes and moves in – he got a villa up the fucking road! Admittedly, it's down in

Fuengirola, but he's coming down to Puerto Banús, getting drunk and driving home. He came off the road and a tree stopped him and his wife Sue going down the canyon; they'd have been dead otherwise. It was lucky – they got out the car and dropped fifteen feet to the fucking ground!

So then they come and tell me that they've bought this flat at the same place where I'm staying. The idea was to keep separate from each other, all along the coast – with Ronnie, Johnny Mason and myself split up, though Mason was next to Everett's place. But Johnny Knight had been arrested, so we didn't want Ronnie living next to me in the Alcazaba.

They came to interview Carlos, the manager of the Alcazaba complex: 'Does Johnny Knight own any property in your development here?'

'No, no, no, no!' he said, so they put all their papers back into their briefcase. They go to the door and he says, 'But Señor Ronnie Knight has an apartment here.'

'Oh, has he?'

So, they turn round and come back and sit down again.

'And his big friend, Freddie.'

'Freddie? Which Freddie's that?'

'Señor Foreman.'

'Oh, *that* Freddie!'

It was the first time my name came into the frame – over him buying a fucking apartment where I was living! This was a long time after the robbery.

That copper is Fred Cutts. He now works down at the Peacock Gym in Silvertown for Tony and Jacky Bowers, doing a bit of charity work with them. But the tactics of my arrest, in July 1989, were totally illegal. They swept me up as I came out of the Alcazaba to buy a newspaper. I was just

walking in my slip-ons to get some groceries and a bit of breakfast. They pounced on me, got me down to Marbella nick; banged me up downstairs. I wanted my lawyer to come down but they never got him for me. They made out he was there so I'd come out of the cell. Instead they got an interpreter down who I'd sold an apartment to.

'Mr Foreman,' he said, 'your lawyer is upstairs.'

Fucking lying bastard! When I went up, I realised it was on top. I was hanging on the stairs, scuffling and struggling. They put the cuffs on me, got me out into the car. I tried to crash the car on the motorway – I knew they were taking me to the airport.

'If you're going to deport me, let me go over to Tangiers, not back to Heathrow!'

But they got me there. As they got me out of the car, I ran round to the departure lounge, over the barrier. They recaptured me and brought me back. We went from the top to the bottom of the stairs, getting on the plane. They got the right needle and were punching me in the bollocks, giving me a hard time.

When I was brought back, the judge said, 'Well, he's here now.'

But my lawyers filed a motion saying I shouldn't be standing there because I'd been kidnapped off the street, brought back without a passport. My lawyers in Madrid were never notified. I'd won a case there: I was a *residencio*, paying two grand a year to be a resident.

The two coppers who came to give evidence against me swore my life away. I supposedly told them that I'd taken part in the robbery and, not only that, but I'd told them Señor Ronnie Knight took part too – that introduced all the evidence from the earlier Knight brothers' trials.

They came and saw me in Brixton and issued this confiscation order for £7 million plus interest. It's ridiculous, but they did it on the others as well, though they'd never get anything back. They tracked down 360 grand of mine on a paper trail from different banks; they traced it from Spain way backwards and managed to come up with that figure.

When Horsley was arrested in 1984, written inside the cupboard door with a crayon they found a similar figure – 300 and something grand, which was deducted from where Horsley had been taking the money out. When they arrested me, they brought this fucking door into the court and stuck it in front of me in the box. All the time they were referring to the similarity to the amount of money they'd traced of mine.

This was how they played their hand – they had no evidence on the robbery charge at all, so it was a backup charge of handling the money. It took them months to find the case of a Chinese guy in Hong Kong who'd been charged with handling. That was the precedent; that they didn't necessarily have to prove the money had come from that particular robbery. Because Hong Kong was under British rule they could use it. My case is now apparently in *Archbold News*, the legal bible, instead of the Chinaman's.

They never even proved it was money from Security Express. There was no evidence to say it wasn't from another robbery, or a drug deal or fraud. I'd also sold the house in Dulwich Village and betting shops to move to Spain; I'd sold a house in America, which I'd had built when I was on my toes there, after Scatty Eddie Watkins shot the customs officer dead during the robbery.

(I'd also left a council flat on the Bonhomie Estate, with Jamie and Gregory living in it – but they'd never paid the rent. I'd left sixty pool-table sites but they were too lazy to get out of bed in the morning to empty moneyboxes. My partner Teddy Dennis had to do it all himself. Fucking hell, I worked hard to get that round together! They blew it up in the air, but that's kids for you.)

The judge gave me a fucking nine-stretch for Security Express, but the jury were shocked; they gasped.

'Where's the beach?' – ironic, eh? I was in Full Sutton prison for a few years until I got down to Maidstone. I was up

at Full Sutton with Eddie Richardson, who was painting a portrait of Lord Longford all the time I was there. I had a visit from a probation officer. I'm only sitting there a few minutes talking when Longford comes over to my table and says to the officer, 'I want to go home now, can you take me home?' because he'd given him a lift there.

So, I said to him, 'Do you mind? We were talking business.' I was trying to get a bit of parole or a transfer down to London because it took visitors all day long to get there. I coated Longford off and told him to piss off out of it.

I went from Full Sutton to Maidstone, from Maidstone to Spring Hill, from Spring Hill to Latchmere. I did a good six-stretch. I think I was on home leave from Maidstone when I met Frank Kurylo and Ian Atkinson (left and right). I knew Frank from way back when he was a minder at Danny La Rue's club. He knew more about me than the average person

and considered it was a story worth telling. The twins had already done two or three books, and you were getting all the different stories coming out. But of course I was always lurking behind the scenes, popping up here and there.

He knew the SP of it, and the underworld of London knew I was always planning things – and what they didn't know they suspected. He and Ian gave me ten grand upfront for my 1997 autobiography, *Respect*. Random House took up the deal and earned well out of it. It was funny – I was on a plane later on, opened this magazine and there were chapters of my book in there.

**FRANK:** Freddie used to come in Danny La Rue's club; he was a regular. I love Freddie. He was a villain, he was the main man, but I used to be a bit wary of him. I'd heard stories of how he'd done this and done that, and I used to call him 'Mr Foreman'.

Later, I saw him in Spain when he had to go there for seven years. I had a pal of mine who was there for twenty-odd years, a right good singer who had a couple of clubs there. I used to see Freddie in Lloyd's nightclub and restaurant, and I'd just nod.

Then I got to know an actress called Helen Keating, who was in *London's Burning*, and I met a girl called June, who had a big house next to Fred's. They both knew him.

Then he got nicked and I got to know him to really talk to when he was in prison. I got a letter from someone who said, 'You've got to get hold of Freddie, he wants to talk to you.'

So, when I gave him my address I said, 'Do you want to do a book?'

There was this millionaire in Leeds called Ian Atkinson, who told me once, 'I want to do a book on the Krays – d'you know enough to do a book?'

I said, 'I've been there, I could finance it, but this is Freddie Foreman.'

'D'you know him?'

So, I said, 'Yeah.' I told a lie because I didn't really know him that well.

Then, a couple of weeks later, he got home leave. We were writing letters to each other, so I met him in the hotel near Marlborough Road station. So, I put it to him: Atkinson wanted to give Freddie fifty grand!

At that time nobody knew much about Fred because he kept everything to himself. Freddie's an extrovert now, but when he was a villain you couldn't talk to him. One fella got a glass eye through him – he'd frighten you to death.

We got the publisher Random Century and a fella called John Lisners. Atkinson was going to give another ten grand to Lisners for writing it. 'But, before this goes any further, before you sign a contract, what's my whack?'

'Five grand,' he said.

'Bollocks!' I said. 'I want twenty grand or you won't get Fred.'

He promised me twenty grand in four lumps, over a year.

Cut a long story short, I'd got cancer by then. I was in bed, about eight and a half stone and no hair. I'd fallen out with Atkinson by this time – he tried to fuck me over the last five grand. He wasn't coming forward because he thought I was going to die.

Atkinson's house was shot at. I got arrested as the fella had used my name as he blasted all the windows and doors shouting – 'This is for Frank Kurylo'

''Ow could I 'ave done anything? I've got no 'air, I'm sick all the time, I've been really poorly for a year!' I said.

'Oh, but you organised it!'

Everybody's ringing up, saying, 'I'm sorry Frank's dead.' Then three years later I had another operation to get some stuff out, and I'm sound. Even the doctor said, 'Fucking hell, I can't believe you're living!'

All of a sudden Atkinson's dead; all the people who think I'm going to die are dead before me and I'm still here. He died of asbestosis from a big factory he used to work in when he was young. Fifty years later it worked on him and killed him.

There's story upon story, upon story, but I got really pally with Fred and we've been pally ever since.

**FREDDIE:** This was my book launch for *Respect*, at the Café Royal, London. Roy Shaw (overleaf, right, with Alfie Hutchinson and me) was a great character. You never knew, when you gave him a drink, whether he was going to eat the glass. He used to munch 'em up! It can't have done him much good in later life, though. He was the original guvnor in the unlicensed boxing game – he beat Lenny McLean the first time around.

At one of those bouts I had a row with the Nashes. I

knocked Tilley, their top henchman on the firm, spark out. They were after my brother-in-law, Freddie Puttnam – he had a row with Roy Nash outside the A&R Club. So, they picked that time to sort Freddie out, at the boxing show when Roy was fighting. We're all mates now, though.

I haven't known Alfie so long, only since I came home last time in the mid-1990s, after the Security Express stretch. But he's a lovely little fella – a good friend of Roy's and an ex-fighter.

I've known Alex Steene, the boxing promoter, for years. I could have gone backstage to meet Sinatra at the Palladium.

I'd just come out of that ten-stretch for Jack the Hat and Alex came running out to my car: 'Come on, Fred, I'll take you back!' But I'd had a drink in the bar with Jimmy Quill (below, with his wife Chris) from The Blind Beggar and Bobby Moore, who Jim was a great friend of – they opened up Morrows, the club in Stratford, together.

Ronnie Kray took a liberty when he shot George Cornell in The Blind Beggar. I said, 'You shouldn't have done that to Jim, that's his front room. The man's family is upstairs.' And they were putting bullets through the fucking floor! Ronnie was all sheepish, but I knew Georgie Cornell and he wasn't

a bad fella. I knew his wife too – Olive Hutton, from south London. Ian Barrie fired a shot into the ceiling and Ronnie fired a shot into Cornell's head. The jukebox jumped and got stuck on the line, 'The sun ain't gonna shine any more . . .'

Bruce Reynolds and me were teenaged mates. His *Autobiography of a Thief* came out before my *Respect*. But Bruce was Bruce – he got me looking at another fucking train after that one, down at Woking!

It was years later, after he'd been released. He came out in his army battledress. I'd gone to the Army Stores to get myself a duffle coat and some boots because we had to go into the woods at night to watch the train come into the station.

It came along on a trolley, but there was security all the way along the platform. It was the early hours of the morning – same old thing, but those trains are coming in from all over the country. I knew about them anyway: they were coming into London and running up into King Edward Building. I was going to have them up in town as they unloaded.

But you couldn't have had it in Woking. I said, 'Look up in the hills' – there were car lights flashing on and off, there were police every-fucking-where! They were surrounding the whole area when that train came into that isolated little station. It was deathly quiet, nothing happening, and they came along the platform with an open trolley with all the sacks on it. That was the money going on board – but I knew that, it was happening all over the place.

In 1997, I took some money and a film crew over to Biggsy. I thought I'd lift him over the wall, just as a joke. I only knew him through getting him out of the country, getting his passports for him, getting him down into Belgium and Paris. Then he went on that little journey. I got a message later to say he needed another passport – he went to Brazil on Ronnie King's.

This documentary was to earn him money because he was skint. Biggsy got five grand for doing a little something. He could live cheaply for fucking months on that; he had a nice little place with a swimming pool.

I always fancied going to Rio and seeing what it was like. This part of Brazil had had the old trams running up the street but they'd all stopped. It was in a state of decay, though it'd seen much better times – the apartments were beautiful, but run down.

Tony Lambrianou (right – seen with Joey Pyle on the left and *EastEnders* actress Gillian Taylforth) was on me because I got him money for a book (*Getting It Straight: Villains Talking*) that the late Carol Clerk did with us.

The photographer came over from New York to take the cover photo in pink shirts – we had a load-up with the shirts and ties. We got about thirty grand – big money, but the police objected to us getting paid for it and there was a big scream in the paper.

Every time he was talking about something with Carol, I said, 'Tony, you got that wrong, that's not how it happened.' He wasn't there – I was there, I know what happened, so let's get it straight, for fuck's sake!

It was while I was living in Shoot-Up Hill that she'd come in my kitchen and work on it. We'd have a bottle of wine.

She liked a lager, Carol; she could put 'em away – she'd match a man.

During that time Martin Fido came out with *The Krays: Unfinished Business* – and that book had all the fucking statements that Tony and Chrissie Lambrianou, Ronnie Bender and these two croupiers had made about Jack McVitie's murder. Tony had sworn that he never – they stayed shtum, him and his brother. They never said anything.

But it came out that they'd made the statements after the trial, but prior to the appeals because Nipper Read and Frank Cater went into Wandsworth late at night. They dotted the *i*'s and crossed the *t*'s. That fucked us on our appeal, Charlie and me. We would have got out because all the lawyers said there was no evidence at all to substantiate what happened.

John Pearson wrote a book on Wilf Pine (overleaf, left, with Charlie's girlfriend, Diane) called *One of the Family: The Englishman and the Mafia*, about how he befriended the Pagano family in New York. They used to come over here and drink with me. Wilf worked with Big Albert Chapman; he started off as a tour manager for Black Sabbath.

The week before Charlie Kray (right) died, Wilf said to me, 'You better get down 'ere, Fred, he's very ill.' It'd be the same before Reggie kicked the bucket – Wilf got us down there.

So, I met Wilf and he took me over to Parkhurst prison hospital on the Isle of Wight. Charlie's leg was like a big fucking balloon, filled with fluid; when he laid his hand on

it, there was an indentation. The heart wasn't strong enough to pump the blood round to the extremities.

During the visit Charlie said, 'I'm sorry for what the twins did to you, and all the aggro they put you through.'

But I just replied, 'You're wrong, Charlie. I did what I did for you, not for the twins. You're my mate.' He had tears in his eyes at this point, so we said our goodbyes.

'The next time you come, bring Jamie down. I'd like to see 'im,' he said.

'Yeah, I will. I'll come down next Wednesday.'

As I got to the door we looked and we both knew it was the last time we'd be seeing each other. I wasn't surprised when they told me a few days later that he'd died.

Charlie was definitely targeted by the police. I was at a cancer charity show with him at the Mermaid Theatre –

there were loads of us there. While I was in the bar there was a little group of guys over by the side. I was introduced to them as ordinary straight businesspeople that Charlie knew. When I looked at one of them there was a moment of recognition. I got the vibe as I shook hands with him; he thought I'd recognised him as a copper. He might even have been involved in one of my cases or arrests because he knew me.

I turned my back and walked away but I looked back and saw their faces: they were undercover coppers, who were setting Charlie up.

So, I said to him, 'Do you know the strength of these people? I don't like the look of 'em.'

'Yeah, they're all right! They've been good to me,' he said. But he was so easily swayed.

I knew a guy who was a car dealer, who had the same problem: Lawrence Gibbons, who had a showroom in Brixton. These coppers came down, who had Northern Irish accents – real bullying bastards. I went down to his office and they were all around him. He got a four-stretch but they set him up with this coke; he got out on appeal. He did two years of his sentence before he won, but he should have stayed in the nick: he went out to have a straight fight with a guy at a party and the guy pulled out a fucking tool, stabbed him to death. He'd opened up a nice showroom down Southend way, with all these American cars, then he had an argument at a party and that was it.

Charlie was a poor bastard, though. To give the man twelve years when he was seventy-two was cruel, but what better scenario than for all three Kray brothers to die in prison? If that doesn't send a message out to the younger generation, what does?

FRANK: When they started doing T-shirts with the Krays' name on, I earned plenty of money out of that. I sent a lot out to Spain, where a load of English lads were – I used to go across with boxes full of them. All the memorabilia was selling, but Charlie was ripping Ronnie and Reggie off, not giving them the money.

The twins wanted him killed. They got £300,000 for *The Krays* film – they should have got a million. Charlie fucked the whole deal up! He got £100,000 of that and fucked over Ronnie's wife, the blonde.

The film rights belonged to Roger Daltrey. Bill Curbishley, Daltrey's manager, did a deal, but it went sour. Daltrey got his money but Charlie went in as adviser and fucked them for theirs – he claimed expenses, he gave some rights away.

He wanted me to buy some rights to a book.

'It'd be a waste of time, and, what's more, *I sold 'em!*' I said.

Charlie was a clown – they used to say that about him: 'Charlie is a Charlie.' He was thick as two pieces of shit! But Freddie will see a different side to him than what I saw.

FREDDIE: I couldn't go up in the witness box and put Charlie down like they all did – Fraser, Lambrianou – saying he was just some mug: 'He was nothing, he was rubbish.' Why call criminals to speak as character witnesses?

'How can they go up there and do him any good? All they can do is harm,' I said.

There are not many photos of Mickey Regan, apart from the ones of us in bow ties in the sixties. This (below) was taken just before he died a few years ago, with my Jamie. He was a great friend of mine. People I met at the funeral told me Mick said, 'You were the staunchest man he ever met.' But I did support him on many occasions.

I'm proud of what my Jamie has achieved, ever since he attended the Italia Conti Academy. I'm so pleased he's progressed in his acting career. He does stage work and tours up and down the country; he's done radio plays, which have been very good; he's done some good film work. They all talk about *Layer Cake*, and then he was in *Elizabeth* and several others. Could have done better on *EastEnders*. He was good on that, but he only signed up for a year's contract, so they had to kill him off in the script!

I've known Howard Marks for years; we did a bit of business together. He said he liked it when the criminal fraternity and me got involved in his deals because no one got fucked

for their money. They were fucking one another left, right and centre! But, with us, everyone got paid.

He always puffs when he does his little turns on the stage – which are quite good, if you see them. He lights up a spliff and has it on the stage, that's part of his act. He'll be with us for many years to come, please god!

This was in Tangiers, in 2010. I got arrested when I went over there to see Tom Hardy, who was acting in the film *Inception*. The Moroccan police nicked me as I was getting off the ferry. They were jumping for joy: it was still on an Interpol notice that I was wanted for a £7 million robbery and there was a fifty-grand reward.

'That was years ago!' I protested.

But they hardly spoke English and I couldn't make myself understood.

My friend was watching through his binoculars. He came down to me with a lawyer. They contacted Interpol and told them I'd already been found guilty of handling money from the Security Express robbery and served a nine-year sentence for it.

Interpol is supposed to be the best police force in the world, but I was clean and it was out of date!

Bruce Reynolds and I were chatting away to Eddie Bunker (left), author of a great crime novel called *Dog Eat Dog*, about prison life and the differences from America; the

privileges you have and don't have; how, out of about three hundred prisoners, you'd associate with only five or six on a daily basis. Ninety per cent are fucking idiots who shouldn't be in there anyway. You've only got a few of your own social standing.

The robbers had the highest standing – not housebreakers, or fucking muggers, or petty criminals. That was against our nature: we only went for the big prizes. Bunker couldn't stand pickpockets, or conmen, or fraudsters.

This boy, Tony Denham (left), out of south London, has boxed, but he's an actor as well. He's been in that comedy *Benidorm*, had other TV parts and was in the film *St George's Day* (2012), with my Jamie. I have him marked down to be one of the firm – Mick or Big George – if a film

or TV series is made of my life. I'd like to give him a turn because he came out to Spain when I put on a boxing show, Spain vs London (we won four bouts and the Spanish also won four). I had the Eltham Boxing Club housed in the Alcazaba and they didn't want to go home. This photo was taken in the Red Pepper restaurant

Christian Simpson (second from left) is my godson. He came over from New Zealand on the eve of his twentieth birthday just as I was being released from the Security Express sentence. He's staunchly loyal, a really big part of my life, and he's fought a few battles alongside me with no sign of fear at all. He's built a great career for himself, working alongside some of the biggest names in the music industry; his protection services are highly respected. He's since married a beautiful Aussie girl named Stacey. I have all the time in the world for her, and for her parents, my Aussie mates Neal and Bron.

Eddie Avoth (second from right), from Wales, was British and Commonwealth light heavyweight champion. John Brunton (right) had the hotel in Norwich where they did all the security arrangements for Reggie Kray. Bill Curbishley put up the money for him to stay there when he was released from prison. That's how I got to know John and he's been a friend ever since.

His daughter had twins of her own, but one of the girls was stillborn. They had to break his little granddaughter's legs and reset her feet; she was also blind in one eye so they operated on it. That's a little fighter! A determined little girl, she's amazing. She's running around now, just got a slight limp. It was weird: she was in a room on her own and they could hear her having a conversation. It was the twin that died: 'She's in the cupboard, I'm talking to her.' Like Reggie and Ronnie Kray, they used to get the vibes: 'I've got to get a message to Ronnie'; or Reggie: 'See how he is.' They had this mental connection. Charlie said, 'It's fucking uncanny with these two, they'll both say the same thing together.'

The same thoughts came into their heads at the same time.

Cliffy Anderson (above, right) was the barman of the Double R club. I nicked him off the Kray twins to work behind the bar of the Prince of Wales, with John Doyland and the other barman. The twins got the hump over that, didn't like it. I've known Cliff most of my life and he also gave evidence for my defence at the Old Bailey. He's my oldest friend; I've known him since the fifties and he still rings me every day to see that I'm ok, or if I need anything.

He fought in the Army Boxing Team as a light heavyweight alongside Henry Cooper.

The others in the photo are the actor Frankie Paul Oatway and my godson Christian Simpson – we were invited as VIP guests to York Hall in the East End to watch some top-quality boxing.

Derek Rowe (below, centre, with former middleweight boxing champion Alan Minter on the right) was a photographer. When I had the Marshalsea he had the top floor as a photographic studio. He used to photograph radiograms and objects for showrooms but he'd also do modelling. I took loads of girls there for photos of them in dresses and costumes – it was a nice little thing if you wanted to sweeten up a young bird.

I saw him years and years later; he just turned up out of the blue and I hadn't seen him since the sixties.

He said, 'I never paid you any rent, Fred, did I?'

But I only charged him a tenner a week because I had the gym underneath and the recording studio. I basically let him have it for nothing because he did me favours. He used to take ringside shots for *Boxing News Illustrated* and send the photos over to *The Ring* in America.

He's a nice guy.

In Australia, my eldest brother Herbie (left – with Wally, who was a para and with the SOE in the war, George and me), who's dead now, used to go to the Army's Colonial Soldiers Society, where he got cheap food and beer. He lived in this club for expats; he was treated much better than he was in this country, they really looked after him out there. He was happy by then, but hadn't always been because he'd lost his little girl when she was twelve years

old – she got polio in her lungs. He kept her off school because she wasn't looking well.

Two nurses were lodging in his house; they got in touch to tell him to come back home and told him that she was dead. He was broken-hearted, and that's when he took his other kids to Australia.

They never came back.

My Danielle (seen here with Jamie and me) has four sons of her own now – including Freddie Junior, who works for Harrods. Danielle, Gregory and Jamie all live over in different parts of Bromley and Beckenham. My Gregory runs the Freelands pub in Bromley.

   Janice King and I have been partners for twenty-six years now. We fell in love out in Spain. My and Maureen's marriage had gone but then I met Janice and it was inevitable that it happened. I still looked after Maureen, even when I came out of the nick. My family have had everything; they've had the best. That's what I did all my time for – providing for them, giving them an education, holidays and homes.

That's Roy Hilder, who's like another son to me, with his wife Sue, standing next to Janice. He was a boxing trainer and manager, down at the Peacock Gym. He's a wheeler-dealer; he's over in Italy, Austria, all round the world and he has a good head for business.

Roy and Sue are my two dearest friends. They met in my pub, The Prince of Wales, for the first time, and that's where they did their courting. I'm in contact with Roy all the time. He takes time out to come and see me – more than most people who should.

For about five years my Gregory and I had the Punchbowl pub in Farm Street, Mayfair, near the big Catholic church. (That's Panamanian ex-boxing champion Roberto Duran in the pub overleaf, second from right, and Pandy, far right.)

It's got a lot of history: they used to have a little court at the back, where they'd pass the booze through this little opening. It goes back to the days of Tyburn.

But now it's changed hands. The filmmaker Guy Ritchie took it over, with a few other people from Prince Harry's mob. They've sold it on to some other people now, but they've kept on the same staff that used to work for us. They've spent about a million quid on it – you wouldn't believe it now. It's a much, much better place than when Ritchie took it over.

There are pictures of him and Madonna out on the pavement with the name 'Foreman' over the top. We were trying to keep it all fucking quiet, but he loved the notoriety! I pitched the film *Bronson* to the two of them

because I'd spent time with Charlie Bronson up in Full Sutton, Yorkshire; I got very close to him.

We used to have little drinks on a Friday night on the food boat. We would get the cheese and biscuits out, pork pies and vodka and tonics. I took him under my wing and it was the best time he had in prison. We used to say, 'Come on, Charlie, your turn to sing!' because we were having a little drink-up. It was only from six till eight because you're banged up at eight o'clock. He'd sing 'What a Wonderful World' by 'Satchmo' (Louis Armstrong) – he'd been in the nick for the past fucking twenty years!

But he kicked off one night – there were a couple of fellows from Wales he had a few words with. They were calling in through the window: 'LGs' (London gangsters) they called us. They were giving him some stick and he smashed up the furniture in his cell. In the morning, they opened up the cell door for breakfast and work but, as we all stood out on the wing, Charlie jumped out bollock-naked, covered in boot polish, with a fucking bandana round his head like Rambo, a broom handle sharpened into a spear in one hand and a leg broken off the prison table in the other!

He has to perform to an audience because all the other prisoners are waiting for him to kick off: 'When's Charlie gonna start?'; 'When's he gonna attack a screw or a prisoner?'; 'When's he gonna get up on the roof and throw all the slates off?'

It's a real shame all of this, because Charlie has a good heart and all he really needs is a break, another chance in life. It's been far too long, and no man should have to go through what he has. If he could just get out of that hell hole then we could have that pint together that we promised each other.

I advised Tom Hardy on his character for *Bronson*, and that's the way he played it in the film. He's made up as a clown: he's got a normal face and then he turns to the other side with a clown's face. That's exactly what I told them and the director made sense of it.

When I saw the vans for the new Krays film, *Legend*, at Pellicci's (the Bethnal Green café frequented by the twins since their youth) I went in there and there was Tom. They'd been rehearsing in there. He was dressed up like Ronnie Kray; he introduced me to Scotch Pat and all the different

characters there. I never asked who would be playing me, or if I'm in it or not – so I don't know and I don't care.

*The Krays* (1990), with the Kemp brothers, was a complete load of rubbish. Let's hope the new Krays film is better than the first. I read the script by Brian Helgeland – I'd taken him down The Punchbowl, had a meal with him because he wanted to do a film with me. But he went back to America and, the next thing I know, he's doing a script on the twins. I suppose he thought that was a better story; fair enough.

But I could see a bit of myself in *The Long Good Friday* (1980) with Bob Hoskins – by virtue of the fact that I went up the river on the boats, raising money for the boxers at the Olympics. I had the pubs. There were a few deliberate fires at the betting shops because of the opposition from people opening shops on your doorstep.

It was a common way of doing it, so long as no one got hurt.

Then there was the cold store where I worked at the meat market, hanging up sides of beef – where they had the faces all hanging up in the film. There was the Irish connection too – I got nicked out in Ireland and wound up in Mountjoy because the IRA put up a bank out there I was going to rob.

Then there was the casino he had that was burnt down, or bombed. Then I was done up on a robbery with a dye gun by a security guard, and I had it coming out the pores of my skin for fucking months! You put the shower on and there was this fucking dye coming out all the time; it took ages to get rid of. People used to come round and say, 'Where's Fred, in the shower?' because I was in there all the time – which they say in the film.

Someone was really feeding them information about me for the character. All of those things came together. I think it's the best film they've ever done about the gangster life.

This is Cliffy Anderson, my godson Christian Simpson and me at Ronnie Biggs's funeral in January 2014 (below).

'So much for compassion, heart and soul – forget it. Ronnie Biggs gave himself up at the age of 71. After suffering three strokes, he could hardly speak . . . [he] had to use a chalk

and slate to communicate to his son Michael. What did they do? Put him in a prison hospital? No, they locked him up in Belmarsh top-security prison. It's bloody disgusting. People complain that the government are soft on crime, but not when it comes to people like myself, or Charlie Kray, or Ronnie Biggs. They'll always find room for us old boys, while preachers of hate, sex offenders and drunk drivers get off with pathetic sentences.

'In my life I've been sentenced to 23 years' imprisonment, 16 years of which I've spent inside 15 different nicks in the UK and abroad, with much of that time in remand for crimes that ended in acquittal.

'Just imagine that, if you will. Those missed birthdays, weddings, funerals, your children growing up, relationships beginning and ending. A whole decade came and went, and when I think about what I missed during that time it saddens me.'

Freddie Foreman in *The Godfather of British Crime* (John Blake, 2007)

*Freddie Foreman in the mid-1960s, with his daughter Danielle. In 1969, around the time of her eighth birthday, he was sentenced to ten years' imprisonment for disposing of the body of 'Jack the Hat'. He would be released in the late 1970s, spending the end of that decade on the run and most of the 1980s at liberty before being captured in Spain, in 1989, on suspicion of committing the Security Express robbery. He was sentenced to a further nine years for handling the proceeds. As Freddie says in his closing statement above, 'A whole decade came and went...'*

Good friends and good company. 5am – and what a night that was. From left: Christian Simpson, Freddie Foreman, Noelle Kurylo and Frank Kurylo at Freddie's apartment in London. This picture was taken by Stacy, Christian's wife.